The ABC'$ of Closing

Experts Secrets to Closing More Deals in Door-to-Door Sales

By Sam Taggart

Published by CKT

CKT

Version 2: Revised 12/10/2018

All closes are to be used in integrity and not for the negative manipulation of consumers. Please practice good sales practices for the dignity and honor of the Door-to-Door Sales industry.

ABC'$ of Closing Video Series

Purchase the full access license to access over 1000 videos on Closing, Leadership, Recruiting, and industry specific content from: Solar, Pest, Satellite, Alarms, Roofing and more. It is one thing to read about sales, it's a whole different experience watching it in LIVE ACTION!!!

We go undercover and film real live sales, role plays, and examples of objections, closes, lines, strategy, mentality and more in Door to Door University. We help over 2000 active users and 50 companies now with their sales training. We have worked with some of the best industry sales professionals, recruiters, and leadership to film content that is dynamic and neutral to serve you and your team.

D2DU is a co-created platform for corporations to build their training program on our platform with preloaded videos. We then consult and support you in uploading your own content that is specific to your needs. We are committed to proving the best training in the direct sales industry, keeping content specific to what we do instead of solely general sales tips.

ABC'$ of Closing has a specific course associated with the book inside, going over each close. Learn the tones used, the pauses, the energy that goes behind each close. Don't just read about closing... watch, listen, and study it. D2DU.com

If you don't want to spend the money, try our FREE version with over 20 free videos!

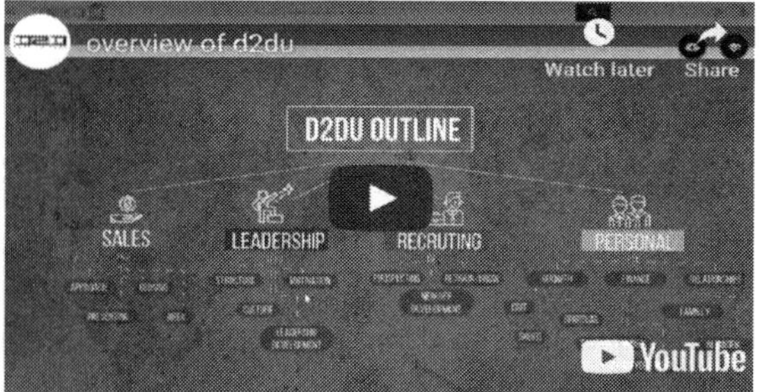

Table of Contents

About the Book

<u>How to Get the Most Out of the Book?</u>

We are supplying you with an arsenal of closes! Meaning when you are in a home you will now have all the ammo you need to make deals happen and in turn COLLECT CHECKS… "Coffee is for closers." If you fail to practice, use and re-use these you will continue to just be the average sales person, getting by check to check. I have sold 1000's of copies of "ABC'$ of Closing" and have had many companies make it a required reading for their sales teams due to results people have seen.

Have you ever read a book all of the way through, and then two weeks later couldn't really tell anyone what the book was even about? This book is not designed to be read straight through – it is meant more so to be used to practice and memorize each close, in order to gradually build up your arsenal of closes.

Short Disclaimer: I can't lay out every possible case and scenario that you may run into while in the field, and I also can't cater this to every product or service out there.

What I HAVE done is created a guide meant to walk you through closes catered to in-home selling, and to teach you how to create urgency, based on my experiences interviewing and working with the best in the business. The psychology behind these methods works, and they are tried and true.

If you haven't already, go subscribe to my podcast "D2D-PODCAST" on iTunes iTunes or soundcloud to find over 100 interviews with the professionals that have accomplished mind blowing feats in their careers. They share abundantly and freely with you on how to become a top performer.

The best way that you can benefit from this is to go SLOWLY through this book, and to make sure to do the exercises so that you can work on building your arsenal of closes. If you are presenting, and you think you can get by with 1-2 good closes and be an all-star, you have it all wrong. I will often use 40-50 different closes throughout one presentation.

<u>Formulate</u>

All of these closes are cross-contextual, meaning that you can make equations to create what I call a "Power Close" or a "Combo Close".

For example:

A+D+B+F = Close
K+T+C= Close

These are to be intertwined and used just as much at the doors as in the home. As you practice them, and they become second nature, you will find that you have become a deadly assassin when it comes to closing. You will know exactly when to pull each one out, and how they can be coupled in the most powerful ways.

Exercises

DO THEM!

Practice

Tip #1 – Go Close by Close

Don't try to learn them all at once. Bite off only as much as you can chew. It is more effective to apply 1-3 new closes into your presentation a week than it is to read the book and try to learn them all, but never really figure out how to apply any of them to your presentation.

Tip #2 – Write it Down

When I was in the earlier years of my career, I wrote down on my hand 1-2 things that I wanted to apply to my day. Throughout that day, the writing would constantly remind me to try them out. Then they would be used over and over again that day and would become second nature, so that I could start adding more and more lines to my arsenal.

Tip #3 – Role Play

Role play with your co-workers. Make sure that your office, your friends, and your managers have all read this book so that you all can be on the same page, and work through it together. One powerful approach according to the book "Grit" by Angela Duckworth, deliberate and disciplined study on your own is the most powerful way to learn and retain knowledge.

A totally different approach would be practicing with a person and working through the tone, the body language, and the speed with which you use them. Apply all of the different learning modalities to this book: read, listen, write, and speak these closes. Before going any further, make sure to get an accountability buddy to start practicing these closes with you. As discussed in The Miracle Morning by Hal Elrod, you learn much more effectively when working with a partner to develop a new skill, rather than trying it out on your own.

Other Resources (page 6-8)

"D2D" is a company to help increase performance for leaders in the direct selling industry. We specialize in developing recruiting programs, leadership development and training for companies in all door to door. To get a FULL experience and to really boost your sales contact us – thed2dexperts.com

This entails start to finish trainings from leaders from all over the country sharing their secrets on what makes a top rep in this industry.

After reading and experiences the shift it will create in your sales performance, I invite you to reach out and see how we can continue to help improve your skills and business, sign up for D2DU or attend D2DCON.

Resources

D2DU – Worlds best collective sales training, helping companies enable their leaders and reps to become top level producers

D2DU.COM

D2DCON

D2DCON – Worlds Largest Direct Sales Conference

D2DCON.COM

D2D-PODCAST – Hundreds of hours, and interviews on Sales, Leadership, Recruiting, and Business

Soundcloud.com/d2d-podcast

D2D Planner – An accountability planner designed to keep you organized and productive.

Recruit-O-Matic – Recruiting CRM, messaging, and accountability platform.

https://recruitomatic.co/

D2D YouTube – Sharing free nuggets, vlog, and tips on how to become a beast in your field.

https://www.youtube.com/c/D2DExperts

D2D TRIBE – Facebook Group which thousands of sales leaders collaborating and sharing best practices.

https://www.facebook.com/groups/D2Dcantknockthis/

@D2Dexperts – Instagram: videos and quotes to keep you sharp on a daily

D2D Consulting – In person and over the phone coaching and consulting. We lift up the hood to your business, and find ways to implement more efficient systems, help build sales teams, and optimize training programs.

D2D Summits - Coaching and networking opportunities, bringing top level producers together to create impactful growth experiences

https://thed2dexperts.com/summit

D2D Goal Boards – Printed goal boards designed to help your sales teams be more accountable.

https://thed2dexperts.com/d2d-shop/

Introduction

If you can't close deals, you don't make money in sales. It's that simple! Many people in direct sales have read countless books on self-improvement, leadership, sales, and so on. These are extremely helpful, and I have gained a ton of knowledge and growth from many of these books myself. The major problem with these books, however, is that most of them never give you an actual transcript of what to say – they just give you the principles. And let's face it – unless you can go make money, and produce, none of that other stuff really matters. Learning principles is extremely important, but sometimes it leaves too much room for imagination.

Additionally, every once in a while, it's nice to just copy and paste what is working for the all-star performers and get the same results yourself. So often reps will try and make up their own methods, when in reality there have been plenty of pioneers that have helped pave the way to success for us. Once I figured out if I just said the same things the greats before me said, I popped off with insane results. I am now passing those techniques to ya'll.

Granted, there is much more to selling than just saying the right things. You must have the right tone, body language, passion, drive, and hustle to make it big in the direct selling game. But the fact of the matter is that if you at least have the script and the playbook, you can start from there. CLOSE, CLOSE, CLOSE!

In this book, I am going to go over 26 amazing key closes that are used throughout different industries, and by a variety of reps, that will help you to close at the highest level possible. I also threw in some invaluable bonus closes that I felt like you just had to know about. These closes are designed to give you an outline, and to help you understand the psychology behind them, so that you can tweak them and apply them to your field. Not every customer, sale, or product is the same. But what I have found in my 17 years in the door-to-door and direct selling industry is that you can use the same closes, just worded differently, with any type of product. The human brain has common reactions to certain things, based on our DNA. If you study the art of persuasion and sales, you will find a common thread throughout all industries and best practices.

My Story

I got into door-to-door sales when I was 11-years-old. My brother convinced me to sell for him door to door. I sold coupon magazines for the local bowling alleys and Jazz games. He was 10 years older than me, and had life figured out. He made $20 for each sale, and paid me $10 to sell them for him, so that he did not even really have work, yet still made money.

When I turned 13, my cousin Peter hit me up and asked if I wanted to try out this new thing he was doing – going around knocking on people's doors to ask if they wanted their address painted on the curb, so that the fire department could more easily find their house. He taught me the basic two-minute pitch, and sent me off. I was hooked. I could sell and paint 4-5 curbs an hour, and charge $20 a pop. As a 13-year-old kid, making $100 an hour, I got addicted to the "sellers high" of the job, and became spoiled on its success. I decided then that no one could dictate what I was worth but me, and never in my life have I worked for a wage.

A year later, I remembered my brother's brilliant scheme to get me to go sell for him, and I convinced 11 of my buddies from high school to go out and sell for me. They charged $20, and I took $8, and then paid them the difference. This was my first taste of door-to-door management, as a 14-year-old CEO: "The Gutterman." We had shirts, a Myspace account – I mean, this was a full-fledged business. For anyone that can't seem to make any money, my recommendation is to go get some stencils and paint curbs. Fast cash, and even a 12-year-old can do it. I learned at a young age, thanks to my parents, that there is no free lunch, and that if you want something, there are many, many ways to go out and earn the money for it. You just have to be willing to go hustle.

When I was graduating from high school, my brother hit me up, because he had a buddy that owned an Alarm Company, Platinum Security. I knew that there was a lot of money in alarms, and I knew that I was going to dominate, because I was slinging like 10 curbs a day on any good day. So, the day after graduating from high school, in mid-June, I shipped off to the lone star state and landed in Dallas, Texas."

My home was always unlocked growing up. I knew absolutely nothing about alarms. Really, I didn't even know a single thing about house keys. I had never talked to, let alone met, the manager in Dallas, because I just asked my brother's friend, Keith, which office I should go to. Keith said to go to D.C. or Dallas, and I chose Dallas, simply because it was closer. I landed on a Friday afternoon, and couldn't get ahold of anyone. I sat at that airport for four hours, feeling nervous because it was my first time away from home. I didn't know a soul, and I didn't have a ton of money saved up. I thought to myself, "This could all just be some stupid joke!" I pulled out my guitar and started to busk in the airport for money, to maybe buy my plane ticket home. I finally got a call from the local manager, Luke, apologizing for running late, because, of course, he was in the middle of a sale.

We drove to the apartments, and I asked him, "What are we doing? Aren't we supposed to get out and start selling?" He was kind of taken aback, because most guys want to settle in, get their stuff together, and then start the next day. But we went straight to turf, and I shadowed him for the last couple of hours of the day. He ended up throwing in two accounts. That night, he said that I had to read a training packet to get travel money, but because I was a lazy 18-year-old, he just pretended that I had read it, and paid me anyway. The next morning, like any good manager would do, he just threw me in the deep end. He gave me three contracts, a shirt, and an area, and said, "Good luck, pick you up around 2:00pm for lunch."

I literally didn't even know how a freaking alarm system worked at this point. I am weirdly good at copying people though, so I just did the same things that Luke had done with the sales that I watched the night before. Did you ever cheat in high school? Well, shame on you. But now, for the first time in your life, it is ok to copy – the better you are at it, the better you will be at this job.

I closed three deals by lunch, and I had to call my manager to ask for more paperwork. Luke was super confused, and thought that I had messed up on all of them or something.

After lunch, I ended up closing two more deals, and on my way home, no one really said anything. We had a rule in the office that when you got back to the apartments, you had to go put your number from that day on the board. We got home pretty late, and I ran in there excited that I had had a decent first day. And when I saw everyone else's numbers from the day, I got super pumped. 0, 1, 2, 1, 1, 1, 3, 2, 1, 0... And then there was me, coming in halfway through the summer, not even at the bottom of the white board – I was on a whole different board because there wasn't room for me. I confidently put up my number five, and went to bed. The next day, everyone in the office was dumbfounded. They were all like, "Who the freak is the new 18-year-old punk who came out of

REP	Wed	Thur	Fri	Sat
Adam				3
Luke				3
Bridger				2
Thomas				1
Matt				0
Shelby				1
Ryan				2
Shawn				1
Ben				1
Tyson				3
Gina				1
Tyler				0

REP	Wed	Thur	Fri	Sat
Sam				5

nowhere and sold five his first day?" I started asking around to the guys, "What do most rookies do their first day? First week? Average day?" They responded, "If you could average one sale per day for your first year that would be amazing." Well, guess how many accounts I sold the next week – FIVE. Those idiots! What they should have done is patted me on the back, hid the number board, and said, "Not a bad first day, don't worry, you'll figure this out sooner or later."

Had they lied to me, gosh dang it, I would have sold 20 or 30 the next week. I was so used to selling 10 curbs a day that I figured giving a free alarm system away wouldn't be much harder. I came out of the gate swinging, a freaking CLOSER, and the best rep out of 11 solid high school kids. Later that year, I learned how to anchor back to the simple fact that *our beliefs dictate our results*.

Lessons From That First Week Selling

Your Mind Dictates Results

Too often we feel we need to know more about the product, have better training, more time on the job, better area, better pricing, etc… The facts are most of selling is mental, or why would have I sold 5 my first day. I had an expectation for myself. You don't just get lucky and close 5 alarms your first day. Train your brain to believe ever door is a deal. Train your brain that you are a CLOSER! Be the sales professional that you would want to buy from Believe you will close deals because you're doing a great thing! We trick ourselves either out of being good or into being something great. Either is up to what we feed our minds, and where we allow our thoughts to go.

Don't Let Others Dictate Your Worth

Just because your manager, office, or friends are selling a certain number, doesn't mean you are limited to that. We tend to conform to the average of those we surround ourselves with always due to the uncomfortable feeling of being too bad, and sometimes too great.

I let the veterans tell me what was normal, and I listened. I didn't have to listen, I could have laughed and said, "I'm sorry that you recruit low level performers on average, but that just isn't how I operate. 5 is my starting point, and I will blow all your records away." I basically did the opposite and apologized, gave myself an excuse to slack off.

The biggest flaw in any sales environment is culture. If you are in a dying culture either get out or be the leader that makes the difference to change the energy of your environment around. Culture creates results or can destroy one's potential.

Copy and Paste

It is that simple… if you can just mirror the exact process of your leaders that are performing well, you will perform. Don't be the rookie that thinks they know everything and do your own thing. Be humble and hungry. We've all heard surround yourself with the best and you'll become the best. That is why I created D2DCON, it's a place where the best come together and share best practices and elevate one another. D2D-Podcast is another way you can surround yourself virtually with the greats, listen and create a relationship with those speakers. D2DU has the best trainers from each industry, nowhere else gives you access to them like our platform.

I switched from painting addresses on the curbs to selling a five-year contract at $49.99 per month, and realized that it is all the same thing! **YOU GRIND, SMILE, CLOSE**! After my first summer in 2008, I served a two- year service mission with the LDS church in Argentina. Boy, was I grateful while there for what I had learned in sales, from knocking on doors. I quickly learned that unlike me, most other missionaries out there had very little experience communicating with strangers. Granted, the Holy Spirit is what converts, but there is an element of persuasion one can have to help bring people into the gospel.

Lessons From My Service Mission

Can't Be Afraid to Talk to Everyone

We were asked to talk to everyone we saw and share our message. People think that selling alarms, pest control, roofing is hard… try changing someone's entire belief system. If you don't open your mouth and share your message, no one hears it. I took that to heart, and made sure I didn't avoid the lady walking her dog, the guy pulling in from a long day at work or old man on the park bench. It's a numbers game, the more people you talk to the more chances you have for success. *More no's = more yeses.*

Routine is Everything

On the mission, you live by an extremely disciplined schedule every day.

6:30am – Workout

7:30am – Personal Study

8:30am – Companion Study

9:30am – Language Study (Sales Specific 😉)

10am – 9pm – GRIND

9:00pm – 9:30pm – Plan and Goal Setting

Following a schedule creates consistent results. Physical fitness keeps your mind and body sharp for the job. Studying is critical to success. Companion study, working with others, role plays, brainstorming and critiquing helps you see your own blind spots, and implement learned skills. Study your craft specifically! You won't die if you're on the streets more than 8 hours. So many reps fail to even work a solid 3-4 hours a day consistently. Come home and review the day, and plan for tomorrow. Write out 3 things you did well, and one thing you can improve on. Then set goals for the next day to keep yourself accountable and on track to your bigger holy cause.

Have Fun and Be You

Often times people have a perception of who they think they need to be in order to get results. The problem is, the second you compromise your own identity you relinquish your maximum potential that you were placed on earth to achieve. Walk in your own shoes. Personalize the scripts. Add your own creativity, and flavor to the sales process. If your funny, be funny. If your serious, be serious and connect with people in that way. I was never afraid to let my light shine on my mission and I had so much fun doing it. I would find other fellow missionaries depressed

because they weren't living their personalities out, and often were lost, having personal identity crisis's. This same thing will happen in sales. You can still live your life, and be you while selling. The sooner you figure this out, the more fun selling is, the better you feel and the better results you will have.

I sold alarms for another five summers after that, and became one of the best alarm reps in the industry. In 2014, I was the #1 sales rep out of thousands for another alarm company, Vivint Inc. – a multibillion dollar companywith the largest door- to-door sales force in the world. This didn't all happen easily – it took a ton of hard work, training, and dedication. I learned quickly how to continue to up-level my own personal standards. I thought that if I was only selling one in a day, what was I doing with the other six hours of the day? Why couldn't I sell two? I then thought to myself, "If it takes me two hours or so to sell two, why can't I do three in a day?" Then, I moved to four a day, and continued to maintain that average. I always root back to the experience of my very first day as an 18-year-old newbie selling five, and I remember that 80% of this is all mindset. If you have the confidence and faith, you will succeed.

In 2015, I left the alarm industry and moved to solar sales, which I was extremely nervous to do. I knew that I was really good at selling alarms, but I knew nothing about solar. It was much more expensive, and had a much longer process. I didn't know anything about solar energy, photovoltaic, inverts, or any of the stuff that went into it. I wasn't even really a treehugger – I had just heard that you could make great money in solar, just like alarms. Before I made the plunge, I decided to try it out a week or so, just to get an idea if I could even sell it.

No one trained me. No one even told me how the things really worked, other than that you save money and energy. My first customer asked me for a card. I didn't have a card.

I took my exact alarm presentation, plugged in solar, applied the same closes that I will introduce you to later, and sold him. I had somehow forgotten the lesson I had learned in 2008, SELLING is SELLING! At that point, I realized very quickly that it didn't matter if I was selling windows, vacuums, makeup, or garbage – I knew that I was a CLOSER! And my first four presentations, I closed.

Now I am going to pass those closes on to you, so you can have a similar experience as I did. You don't have to go through the same hardships I did, you can skip a lot of the learning curve and start making money a lot faster by having this book. Take the nuggets I share serious and I promise you will start seeing results.

CLOSING 101

Brian Tracy's definition of a close is, “Anything that gets you closer to the end of a sale is a CLOSE”.

I have always viewed closing as a funnel, versus pushing someone off of a cliff.

You start super wide, and then you slowly wind them down into more of a focal point, where they are signing and giving payment information. We call this using a series of **Soft Closes.** The common mistake that reps make is that their process looks a lot more like this: They just push them along this path, then right off of a cliff, and hope the customer is OK saying yes. There is no building of trust, no soft closes, no checking their temperature to see where they are in the process. This never ends well. We call this **Hard Closing.**

In our industry, it's extremely important to learn a myriad of soft closes, because we show up at random, and have zero rapport with most everyone we're working with. It is going to take them a second to warm up to you, and to the idea of buying something right on the spot.

Let's say you were to only have one close rehearsed, you try it, and it doesn't work… now what? You need to practice using lots of closes throughout your sales process and have backups upon backups.

Closing is Honorable

Don't be ashamed of pushing someone into a decision. People tend to shy away from commitment and without quality sales people the market would be stagnant. Believe in what your selling, much more than the customer will ever initially believe in it. They will naturally push back on what you're selling, but you need to see past that and imagine 3 months or 3 years down the road when that service is making a big difference in their lives. You act as the catalyst for change and value in their lives, and should take pride in that, not shame yourself for taking your profession as a "CLOSER" serious.

Believe in Yourself

The fastest way to succeed is to simply change your mindset going into the close. Many reps don't even believe that they are going to get the deal when they walk in. Go in with full intention that you are going to make the deal happen no matter what. You should be more surprised when the customer says no versus when they say yes.

OBJECTIVE > OBJECTION

Sales are 100% in your control. Reps think they can't sell because of the product or the area. But the fact of the matter is, more often than not, it is just the one presenting it. You must take more ownership over your results in order to have better results. There are a ton of reps that sell based on chance. They credit all of their success to luck, and never fully consciously figure out what made the sales happen. The best reps out there can knock right behind the average rep all day, and pull out deals.

Below is a simple way to look at how you perceive your day selling, and the difference between low level reps and top reps. Obviously, based on your industry, these numbers may vary.

Rep	Acts Per Day	Level of Excitement
	0	Hating Life
	0	Expect It
Low Level Rep	1	Happy
	2	Ecstatic
	3	Buying everyone Drinks

Rep	Acts Per Day	Level of Excitement
Top Reps	1	Hating Life
	2	Expect It
	3	Happy
	4	Ecstatic
	5	Buying everyone Drinks

Believe in Your Product

Believe in what you're selling. Too often, we stop ourselves from selling simply because we are nervous that it won't benefit the customer. Make sure to find out all of the little things that your product or service can do to really impact your customers lives immediately, or someday down the road. It's your responsibility to sell each customer. The customer is on the defensive 99% of the time, and will tell you why they don't want it. They will initially have walls due to lack of trust, and skepticism. *Sell or Be Sold*, by Grant Cardone, talks a lot about the concept that either the customer sells you, or you sell the customer.

Get to a Closing Position

Many people fail to be in a position to get a sale. Most sales require both spouses present. Often times its best to be sitting down at a table. Be in a position where you can present things to them, instead of trying to just talk about them from the couch across the room. If you're in the living room there may be times where you need to get up and show them things. Get cozy with them on the couch next to you. Get the decision makers present. Remove or deal with all distractions: TV, kids screaming, cooking, guests, etc...

Pre-Frame

The power of a good pre-frame will also help with this. A pre-frame is when you set the stage at the beginning of the presentation. You let them know what is going to happen in your presentation, what you expect from them, and what they can expect from you.

For example:

Example 1) "To make the best use of your time and mine, we are going to quickly go through how this program works, what it costs, and why it would benefit you. At the end, if all the numbers make sense, then we start the process today. If not, then hopefully you can point me to the people this will be the right fit for."

Example 2) "I'm not the card or flyer guy – I don't like to play the back and forth, back and forth, with emails and a million visits. And I'm sure you don't like that either. My whole job today is to answer all of your questions, and see if this is a good fit for you guys, or not. If it is, which I believe it will be, great – we get everything rolling. But if it's not, no big deal."

Example 3) "I'm not the guy that sets up appointments – I'm the one that actually has all of the facts and figures to make this happen today. So, if everything makes sense at the end, we do it. If it doesn't, then we don't. No biggy."

Another way to use a pre-frame looks like this:

At the beginning of your sale, when the buyer's resistance is high, explain that you are just going to show them why other people have bought and what they liked most about it. Then, let your customer decide for themselves one way or another if they like it or not.

"I'm just going to go through why others in your area have bought, what they have liked most about it, and if they continue to get it. I'm not going to try to sell you anything. At the end, I'll let you judge for yourself whether or not this fits your needs or interests. All I ask it that you listen with an open mind, and at the end let me know one way or another if this is a good fit or not. Is that fair?"

You get them to agree to make a decision right up-front. Then at the end, you can say something like:

"Mr. Jones, you promised you'd give me an answer one way or another, and from what you have been saying it seems like this is ideal for your situation." Then go on to close them!

Ask Don't Sell

Too often, reps don't focus on doing what's called a "needs audit." This is where you figure out what the customer's problems are, and what would really benefit them. Often times, we push a product or service down a customer's throat that they don't necessarily need or want. It is our job to bring needs and wants out of the customers, and the best way to do that is by asking quality questions. Unless you know what the customer wants, you are never going to close deals.

Here are a few great questions you might try at the beginning of your sale, in order to discover the needs of your customer:

- "What is the main thing that you're looking to get out of our visit?"
- "What interests you the most about our product or service?"
- "What exactly are you looking for?"

- "Which of these stands out to you the most?"
- "What have been some of your biggest frustrations with your current service/product?"
- "Why did you let me in?"
- "Hypothetically, if you were to get this, what about it would you like the most?"

Close! Don't Present

Closing is not presenting – closing is moving the customer along a journey to a decision. Many reps get into presentation mode, where they just throw-up a great deal of facts and features all over the customer. Customers soak in the facts, and then thank the rep for their time and move on. This is probably the most frustrating place to be in as a rep, when you are giving many demos, but not making any money.

I once had a rep who I liked to knock a week behind. My reasoning was that he was amazing at warming the customers up, was so nice, had great charisma, and was truly good at getting people interested. He sold very few accounts, though. I asked him if he was done with that area, and when he said "Yes," I would then proceed to go follow through his turf. And I always sold the lights out. One day, I decided to call him and let him know that I had closed quite a few of the people that he had met with, and that they told me to tell him "Hi." He got pissed! I simply asked him why he didn't close them, when they were begging me for it. And the fact of the matter was that he always failed to ASK FOR THE SALE!

Don't be that guy! If you are leaving, and you don't get a YES or a NO from your customer, you are doing something wrong. Never shoot for a MAYBE.

Don't Fear Rejection

Believe it or not, some reps fail to close a deal simply because they don't want to hear "NO". I would rather hear the word "NO" than "Let me think about it," or "We will get back to you." I walk into a deal expecting a YES, and if it isn't that, then I want a NO. Rejection is all a part of this job. The moment you can accept it, process it, not take it personally, deal with it, and then let it pass, the sooner you can actually start calling yourself a closer. Rejection does nothing to you – it doesn't hurt physically, and it won't harm your family. But too many people get so scared of it that they are literally crippled, and they have anxiety so high that they can't even get out of their car door to go knock.

Fear is the biggest thing that stops people from succeeding in this job. If you asked people why they don't do door-to-door, and if they answered you honestly, 99% would admit, "Because it's too hard to handle all of the rejection." This job is not that physically hard. You walk around a neighborhood all day. But it is a mental battlefield every day. I can guarantee you that the best rep on this planet still gets the butterflies while driving to areas, and they still experience fear of the unknown every day. The top reps probably deal with more rejection than you do. The top reps have to deal with everything the low-level reps deal with, but it is how they respond that makes them different.

Responding to rejection is very simple. *Selective amnesia*. Forget it, and move on. If you carry the weight of every no on your shoulders all day, yours will be a sad, sad story by the end of the day. Your energy will be sucked dry, and your confidence will be shot. Pretend your Dory from "Finding Nemo" knocking doors. If someone were to be the ultimate jerk to her, that very next door she would be back to same old dory not remembering what happened on the last door.

You need to be able to realize that the customer is not rejecting you as a person, and they aren't even rejecting your product most the time – 90% of the time, they are rejecting the fact that you are someone showing up to their home trying to sell them something, and they don't like to buy things. MOVE ON, and **realize that every door is a brand-new opportunity**, and the customer behind that door didn't see what happened at the last door. We often think that the next home we're about to approach was watching us get our face kicked in by their neighbor, so we show up to their home that way.

In sales, the easiest time to get a sale is right after a sale, because your confidence is then sky high. Well, that goes the other way too – the hardest time to get a sale is right after you didn't get a sale. And that is a heck of a lot more common than getting a sale. You have to switch your mindset to walk around as if you have been selling everyone – it will make your job much easier. I think of it as almost tricking our own minds into believing something that isn't. I call it self-inflicted faith. If we tell ourselves something enough times, we will start to believe it. This is where the power of affirmations kicks in – positive self-talk makes a world of difference when you are in a battlefield of rejection and self-doubt.

Ask for the Sale

The most common mistake that reps make is that they fail to ask for the order. When I have trained other reps, I've watched this happen countless times. No matter what else happens, always ask if they want to buy at the end. It may come off as sloppy or awkward, but if you never ask, the answer is always no. Never walk away from a door without asking for something. Even from the people that tell you no, you can at least get referrals, a glass of water, or information about the area. Asking is not rude. You must get over the uncomfortableness that naturally comes from asking for something from someone. Your job is to ask people to buy, and the sooner you get over the awkwardness, the sooner you can become a top performer.

<u>8 Mile</u>

In the final rap battle of the movie “8 Mile,” featuring Eminem, Eminem took a different route than what was typically done in a rap battle. He bashed on himself, instead of on the rapper he was battling. Often, people aren’t expecting us to know the common objections, so they bring them up. But if we spearhead them before they come up, it leaves the customer speechless, and makes the sale go much smoother, with far fewer objections along the way.

*This guy aint no mother-f$&%*n MC,*

I know everything he’s got to say against me,

I am white, I am a f$&%# bum, I do live in a trailer with my mom,

My boy Future is an Uncle Tom.

I do got a dumb friend named Cheddar Bob who shoots himself in the leg with his own gun,

I did get jumped by all 6 of you chumps

And Wink did f&0 my girl,*

I'm still standin here screamin "F&* THE FREE WORLD!"*
Don't ever try to judge me dude

You don't know what the f(& I've been through*

But I know something about you

You went to Crankbook, that's a private school

What's the matter dawg? You embarrassed?

This is guy's a gangster, he's real name's Clarence

And Clarence lives at home with both parents

And Clarence's parents have a real good marriage

This guy don't wanna battle, He's shook

'Cause there no such things as half-way crooks

He's scared to death

He's scared to look in his f$^%&$ yearbook, f$%& Crankbook

F$^% the beat, I go acapella

F#$% a papa doc, f*%& a clock, f$%$ a trailer, f%&$

everybody

F#$^ y'all if you doubt me

I'm a piece of f#%ing white trash, I say it proudly

And f$$ this battle, I don't wanna win, I'm outty,*

Here, tell this people something they don't know about me.

There are **4-5 common objections** any door-to-door guy gets **when knocking:**

- "Not interested."
- "I'm busy."
- "Can't afford anything."
- "Someone has already stopped by."
- "I already have it."

The first 30-seconds of your approach could simply squash these objections, so that it makes it extremely difficult for your customer to come up with a way to kick you off of their porch. Here would be a simple example of what I mean:

"Hey, sorry to bother you, I'll be super quick, don't worry I'm not here to sell you some crazy 5000 vacuums (or whatever). I do _______ and I know you probably have talked to a million other _____ over the last little bit, but that is exactly why I'm here. What I do is totally different...."

"Hey, I'm ____. I'll be super quick. I know you probably hate all the guys that come to your door trying to sell you crap, don't worry I'm not like those guys, I don't like them either. What I do is _____.

"Hey, I see that you have ______. That is the reason I stopped by, we look for people that already have _____."

You can also "8 Mile" people in the home. Same thing – people are going to have common objections that will come up in your presentation, and you should make sure to bring them up smoothly and turn them into benefits, before they can bring them up. It is better to be pushing rocks down the hill instead of pushing them uphill.

Common objections you'll get with most products **in the home:**

- "Can't afford it."
- "Need to think about it."
- "Do you have a card?"
- "Let me shop around."
- "Let me research your company."
- "This sounds too good to be true."
- "Don't have the money now."
- "Already have a company."

It's important to use your intuition in the home to foresee these objections. Read your customers body language, tone and responses to predict potential objections so you can 8 mile them easier. You should craft one-liners to use throughout your presentation in order to squash them early on.

These are a few simple lines you can use throughout your presentation to "8 Mile" these common concerns. I would recommend being proactive, and strategically inserting these into your sales presentation.

"The reason why most people get this from me is because they are tight with their money and on fixed incomes, and they figured this would be the most effective way to save money..."

"Most people ask for a card, and a flyer at the end, but I don't do that, just to let you know. I have a lot of area to cover and it is extremely hard going back and forth to every home when I do everything on foot." (Knocked on Your Door close page 119)

"What's cool about my program is that I show you different options that are out there in comparison to mine, just so you know that you're getting the best deal. You wouldn't want to overspend on something like this, and would want to know you're getting the best bang for your buck, right?"

"Fair warning, most people say this sounds too good to be true, but the fact of the matter is that I couldn't be doing anything too crazy or a ton of your neighbors wouldn't have already done this." (Bandwagon close page. 51)

"Most people's concern when I come to their door is how am I going to buy anything when I am already tight right now with my budget, but our program makes sense for anyone's financial situation, don't worry, that is the best part.

"Now I know most people don't like to CHANGE... But at the end of the day this always makes sense for people in your situation. Trust me, I see it all the time."

Leverage Your Arrows

There is a lot of power in holding your arrows until the end. If you start by offering your price high, then giving some ability to come down and negotiate, it will help your customers feel as if they won the negotiation. You need to have arrows to pull out of your quiver towards the end that could help push customers over the edge. You can throw in an extra month for free, offer another free feature, drop the price a little more, or have an additional product you can throw in, and so on. The key to this is to hold back enough arrows at the end so that when the customer wants to negotiate, you are ready for it, and can make them feel as if they "won" the negotiation, and you had to cave-in. Don't cave super easily – make it hurt when you do cave, and show that. If they sense that they have milked you dry, they will stop and make a decision to move forward. It is rare for someone to go through the hassle of winning a negotiation and then not move forward. So, realize that if you can find the right offering for them, they will make a purchase.

CLOSES

ABC'$ OF CLOSING

Assumption Close

Stating things as if they have already happened, or with 100% certainty that they are going to happen.

(Similar to Ownership Close page 148)

You speak and manifest an outcome through the assumption close. This close is all about your state of mind and the energy you bring, versus the words you're saying. The first step in your approach is to talk as if they have already bought from you. This shows confidence, and engraves in the brain of your customer, and yourself, to have "CLOSE" in mind. Speaking confidently and using assumptive language creates energy and excitement in your sale. Showing up this way becomes contagious. Assuming is an art – when you assume, it needs to come off natural, not forced. If your customer feels bullied or pressured, you will lose rapport, and, most likely, the sale.

The assumption close is a subtle way to transfer ownership of the product to your customer. Used properly, your customer will now imagine themselves with the benefits of owning your product or service. Helping customers use their imagination will produce powerful purchasing desire!

Transfer of ownership examples:

"Your savings", "your system", "your equipment", and "your production.

You should use this type of language from the beginning to the end of your sale.

Assumptive language example:

- "The installer will let you know how to use your equipment when he gets here."
- "After your install, I'll follow up and ask for referrals."
- "We will put your sign right here by the flower bed."

A few words that are commonly used in assumption communication are:

- After_________
- Your ________
- When the________
- Once you_________
- When you decide_________
- This will ________
- You will ________
- We will _________

Reps that talk in a passive voice, or come across as uncertain will create passive results and uncertain outcomes. Being assumptive can be uncomfortable, and you may feel as if you are coming off as cocky or arrogant. These feelings are totally normal, and will go away with practice. As the saying goes: you'll lose 1 out of 5 for being *too* assumptive, but you get the other 4.

Exercise:

Write down 3 ways you can use the assumption close in your sales process.

____

____

____

____

____

____

____

____

____

____

____

____

____

Bandwagon Close

Utilizing outside influences to create a sense that "Everyone is doing it."

Have you ever felt buying pressure because others you know already bought? Using the bandwagon close creates a sense of FOMO (fear of missing out) in your customer's mind. This creates urgency, and leads them to make a buying decision. This can be used on the door or in the home in many different fashions. It gives validation and legitimacy to your offering, because no one wants to be the first to act. Realistically, most customers won't take the time to research your company, offer, or product. With bandwagoning, they can assume that others already spent the time researching, so that they are safe to buy. Humans have a natural need for approval, which leads to one of two outcomes:

1. Customers sense that the community isn't buying, and that they won't fit in if they were the only ones doing it.

2. Customers sense that the community is buying, and that they would be missing out if they didn't act on your offering.

Top performers bring to their neighborhoods a momentous atmosphere that creates a feeling as if everyone is doing it. They know the names and backgrounds of their customers and the key influencers in the area, and leverage them in their approach. This is very effective when combined with the Intelligence Close (page 105).

Stories create emotion, and are the best way to bandwagon. They build a bridge between your customer and someone they trust and can relate to. This is astronomically more powerful than pitching them on only features and benefits. You must have an arsenal of stories that can be weaved throughout your pitch, in order to effectively overcome common customer objections.

When using a story, you can be much more blunt and bold about getting your point across. You can place all pressure and responsibility on the third-party prospect, but, inadvertently, you are influencing your current customer. Stories create authenticity, realness, and emotions.

When you use a story the right way, it will come across as if their neighbor is pitching them, not you. You just happen to be the middleman relaying the message. This can be used with the "Feel Felt Found" Close as well (page 82).

Never make up or misrepresent people in your area, as it can come back to bite you in the butt. Realize that people talk after you leave, which can ruin your reputation in an area. If you don't have customers or stories, make more of an effort to create business, and get the ball rolling. Talk with others in your office to collaborate stories to create fast momentum.

Try to use stories of familiar neighbors that customers should know, but if you don’t have any, you can say things like, "John Smith, he lives just north of here, he is also an engineer and his favorite part was ____." North of here could mean 10+ miles north in your last area. Still effective, but if they knew John Smith, it would be more effective.

Another effective way to really use this close is by asking your customers to write or record a testimonial. I have books of 3 by 5 cards that have testimonials of why customers bought from me, and what they loved most about it. It is also powerful to have them put down their major concern, and how you overcame it.

Never make up or misrepresent people in your area, as it can come back to bite you in the butt. Realize that people talk after you leave, which can ruin your reputation in an area. If you don't have customers or stories, make more of an effort to create business, and get the ball rolling. Talk with others in your office to collaborate stories to create fast momentum.

Try to use stories of familiar neighbors that customers should know, but if you don’t have any, you can say things like, "John Smith, he lives just north of here, he is also an engineer and his favorite part was ____." North of here could mean 10+ miles north in your last area. Still effective, but if they knew John Smith, it would be more effective.

Another effective way to really use this close is by asking your customers to write or record a testimonial. I have books of 3 by 5 cards that have testimonials of why customers bought from me, and what they loved most about it. It is also powerful to have them put down their major concern, and how you overcame it. When customers have a major concern, you can then leverage these cards.

Here's a way to ask for a written or recorded testimonial:

> "I'm going to have you guys write a testimonial at the end of this stating the biggest concern you had with getting the system, and how I was able to earn your business and solve the problem. So tell me the main concern that is holding you back so we can get this going."

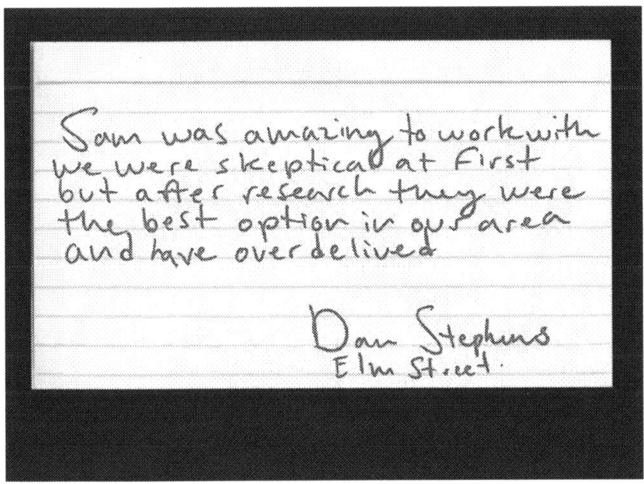

Notice how I used an Assumption Close and was able to pull out their main concern.

Filming their testimonial is super powerful, because people can put a face to a name. You can show people that are local, in their area, and show why they got it. Faces also help create credibility.

Bandwagoning has EXTREME power in D2D sales. It can be one of your strongest ACEs to getting into homes and closing deals. Knock without bandwagoning, and you're a complete stranger. But when you can build a bridge, and show that you know people that they know, you become part of their network and can then be trusted. I've even had people think I lived down the street from them.

> "You guys are just like the Jones's! They also have 5 kids, and wanted to be able to check in on the all the chaos while they are away..."
>
> "You know the Johnsons next door, right? They also did it because they have been looking for an affordable way to get their yard done with a reliable company. Then after looking for a while, with extensive research, they found we were the best price and best quality."
>
> "Have any of your neighbors told you what is going on?"
>
> "Have you seen my trucks at your neighbor's homes? Like Bill, Steve, John, etc...."

> "Do you know anyone on this list? (Hand them a list of people you have set up.) Yeah, all of these people have already done what I'm doing. So, obviously I'm not doing anything crazy… So, what I did for them is____ …"

Exercise:

Write down 2 stories or examples of customers you have sold or someone you know has sold that you can use to overcome a common concern and create emotion.

____

____

____

____

____

____

____

____

____

Competition Close

Creating buy-in from your customer to help you or your company accomplish something of greater purpose. Different forms of this could be sales competitions, prizes, accomplishments, or goals. Include the deadline, and what it would mean to you.

Sales is a GAME. The more you treat this job as a sport the more money you will make. Our whole lives we have been trained to provide an income in order to meet our needs. Problem is sales doesn't pay based off what your needs are, it pays based on how you produce. Often times we get complacent because we make money so quickly and our needs are met. This is a slippery slope that will lead to mediocre results. The fastest way to prevent average results is to make this job into a competition. Stop looking at your paychecks and start looking at the scoreboard. Are you the top rep? How are you winning or losing? I promise your results will skyrocket when you find someone or something to compete against.

Top reps realize that competitions can be used to motivate prospects to buy. Sales companies create competitions to motivate sales reps through recognition, prizes, milestones, trips, etc. When you share what you are fighting for, and why, there is a sense of empathetic participation invoked in your customer – people naturally want to help. If done right, and done authentically, your customer will buy into you and will be more inclined to say yes.

You have to give them a good reason to buy now. Under normal circumstances, there are few reasons for a customer to make a same-day decision. But the competition close creates a sense of urgency, and they will be more inclined to buy. You can bring them into your world by saying things like:

"This is one of the last few days in my tournament."

"I would be letting the whole team down."

"We would potentially forfeit a trip to Hawaii if we don't do this now."

Reps often are ashamed of customers knowing about their success and personal lives. We also fear letting them know how our job and company works. It isn't bad to open up to your customers, and have them buy into your cause. You will find that this will help you become more of a real human that deserves to be treated with compassion and respect, versus just a scummy salesman. Show them pictures, stats, dashboards, social media posts, prizes, or reports. This kind of authenticity will invite your customers into your life. People want a BADASS rep to sell them. No one wants to buy from someone that doesn't have a desire to win, or to serve at the highest level possible. Remember being a "Closer = Closer" to one's ambitions.

How to use the competition close the right way:

1. Ask for permission

   "Hey, can I share with you a goal of mine?"

   "Wanna hear what I'm competing for right now?"

   "Can I ask for a huge favor from you?"

2. Explain the competition or goal in an emotional way

"For the last 3 years, I have had a goal to finish Top 10 in my company. As an award, they get an all-expense paid trip to Europe! The last 2 years I was in the top 50 out of 500, but this year I am ranked 15th. I know if I put in extra hours and serve my customers at the highest level, I can make Top 10. This year they are going to Italy, and that has been a dream of mine since I was a kid, because my heritage is from there. If I get 10 more deals by the end of the month, it should put me in the top 10. LET'S GO!"

"We are in a sales tournament right now fighting to win a _____, and our whole team here in Las Vegas is neck-and- neck competing against our biggest rivals, the L.A. Team. Think of the biggest rivalry in college football, like USC versus UCLA, or something like that. If we win, our office will go on a cruise to Mexico, and there are only 2 days left. My whole team is counting on me to pull my weight, and I really don't want to be the ONE guy that costs us the whole trip. So, what do we have to do to make this happen?"

"My goal is to do two more deals on your street today."

It is extremely important to make your customer feel as if they are a key part of the team, and you're both competing against the opposing: office, sales rep, or company. By portraying this to your customer, with assumptive language, you can create an empowering atmosphere and can enroll the customer into winning with you! Focus on a win-win – no one likes to lose.

Note: make sure this is genuine and it isn't made up. If there isn't a Europe trip, or you're not from Italy, then don't say that. Top reps create daily/weekly/monthly goals, and are completely aware of their progress towards their goals. They also know that their performance increases during competitions. With that knowledge, they will religiously throw- down with others in the office or company. At the very least, share your personal production goals with your customer.

3. State that you know it doesn't mean much to them, but it means the world to you

4. Ask for the deal

"What do we need to do to make this happen today?!"

"You know you are going to get this one way or another, how about we make it happen now? It will make a big difference for me."

"Because of this competition, I will knock ___ off of the price today. That's how committed I am to winning this! Let's do it!"

As a rep, it's your responsibility to be 100%convinced that everyone could benefit from your service, and that is the reason you are out selling it. If you doubt it, your production will suffer, and you will soften up when customers give you resistance.

Exercise:

Write down 3 things you are fighting to win/accomplish this quarter you could use in this close to create emotion.

1)____

____

____

____

____

2)____

____

____

____

____

3)____

____

____

____

____

Bonus Close

Change Places Close

- Having the customer put themselves in your shoes in order to find out their main objection or hesitation, and move forward.

> "Mr. Jones, put yourself in my shoes for a second, and let's suppose you were talking to someone you really knew would benefit from this service or product, and they just wouldn't tell you what their main hesitation was for not moving forward, what would you do in my situation?"

> "If roles were reversed and you were selling me, tell me why this would make sense"

Now, most of the time the customer will then just tell you what is holding them up. Resolve it, and then close. Another way is simply to ask them:

Rep: "Is it the money?"

Customer: "No, it's not the money."

Rep: "Well then, can I ask you what is holding you back from making a decision?"

Customer: "OBJECTION."

Rep: 1) Solve objection

2) Ask for sale

Discount or Deal Close

Giving the customer a special deal to get them to make a decision now.

Naturally, people don't like to be sold. Deals such as "buy one, get one free," or "Memorial Day special" are used to relieve buying pressure and to help people make buying decisions. Everyone gets skeptical when being sold, and they want to know that they're getting the biggest bang for their buck. We constantly validate purchases by checking prices online or by calling a trusted friend/expert. There are even times when we won't buy something simply because we think that the product may be better priced in the future.

If you get in the habit of Give - Give - Give, you won't ever be an effective closer. Top reps always practice the **give and take method**. If a customer is asking for a lower price, a free month, waived activations, or so on, and you are willing to do it, you need to ask for something in return. This can be as simple as a banana for the road, or a glass of water. My go-to ask is always for referrals. The best way to do this is before you say yes to lowering the price, or whatever you do – make sure to set some ground rules as to what you need in return in order for you to offer the deal. Later, I'll demonstrate what I mean by this, and how it can lead to a close simply by doing this the right way.

Be extremely careful of getting into the habit of giving away the farm. This is the lazy way of closing. Forming this habit actually makes you weak as a closer, and in the long-term, you will sell less. It is better to utilize the offering that you were going to give in the first place in order to leverage on deal giving, versus giving them a killer deal, and then entering into negotiation. By not doing it this way you will really eat into your commissions. Stay true to your values on what you believe is fair. I have walked away from some customers that have flagged me down 1 week later saying that they thought about it, and want to buy, because I had originally told them that if they get this now I would waive their initial payment, and if they wanted to buy later, I wouldn't do that. I had to stay true to that statement.

Remember, though, a deal is better than no deal, even if you only make a little on it. The main reason being that it will help you get another name in the area, and, if done right, get referrals on it. Sometimes people care too much about the commission versus the number – if you are in the business of winning, and selling lights out, don't be afraid to care more about the number versus how much you make on each deal. You will end up selling more deals anyway with that mindset, but remember to be conscious of what you truly are making and losing on each deal. Make sure you are profitable on all your sales.

Understanding the "Arrows" technique mentioned on page 32 is key to maximizing this close.

Example 1:

> Customer: "Look, we just don't have the money today to pay for the activation. We would do it if we didn't have to pay anything upfront."
>
> Rep: "Well, we have this in place for _____ and it is part of the company's program, but if I can make a deal for you, are you open to it?"
>
> Customer: "Of course."
>
> Rep: "If one, we can get this thing done today and we make the rest of this process quick and smooth. And two, you give me 4 names of people in your network that would also benefit from this service, then I will pay for your activation. I also have rules on the 4 names. You have to introduce me

and them on a group text. Deal? (Does that sound fair)?"

Note: This is an opportunity to take charge again and to set the terms of the deal. Make the terms based on what you are trying to accomplish. If they agree with your mini agreement, they will for sure agree to the overall purchase.

Example 2:

Rep: "What would make this deal a win for you? I'm not making any promises, but if you could have it your way, what would sound fair?"

Customer: "If it was more like $40 per month I would do it."

Rep: "Hypothetically, if it was $40 per month right now, today, there wouldn't be any other things getting in the way for you to make a decision right now?"

Customer: (May go one of two ways.)
1) "Well, I would still want to research it and ask my wife...."
2) "No, I would do it."

You now just figured out if price really was the issue, or if there were other concerns behind it. You can at this point begin the negotiation, and give them a deal that is a win-win for you and for them. You don't want to make the mistake of negotiating yourself down when price isn't really the concern.

Exercise:

Write out what types of deals you are willing to give to customers.

____

____

____

____

____

____

____

____

____

____

____

____

What deals are you already giving that you aren't leveraging to create value?

Bonus Close

Door Knob Close

- After giving the sale everything that you've got, the customer is still telling you no.

1) Pack up all of your stuff, and start walking out.

2) As you go to leave, grab the door handle– when pressure is totally off the situation, look back, and ask, "Jim, can I ask you one last question? What was the main reason you didn't move forward today? Just for the sake of my learning."

The customer will then reply with their concerns.

You'll say, "Freak, why didn't you say so...", and overcome the dang concern while walking them back to the table and locking that thing.

Excuses/Explanation Close

Changing their "excuse" from why they can't buy, into an explanation of why their "excuse" is the main reason to buy.

People have been conditioned their entire lives to believe that being sold is bad. It's associated with negative experiences, and a feeling that we will get in trouble for spending money frivolously. People are also conditioned for instant gratification, meaning that when they want something, they will go out and purchase it. Sometimes there is good reason for certain purchases. But other times, we completely justify bad spending. Great sales reps are so convinced of their services, that they persuade people to justify the close through their enthusiasm. If you create enough value and desire for your service, they will buy!

Think about it – as Americans, we are conditioned to live on credit cards, to get immediate gratification, and to keep up with the Jones's. We need to use the same trigger words that customers tell themselves when they are window shopping at a mall. They go in with zero expectations of buying anything, then walk out of the mall with $100 worth of clothes. People make excuses for why they need things all the time.

- "Just this once."
- "But it's on sale."
- "This is worth it."

- “This is a one of a kind.”
- “I will use this ALL the time…”

When they give you an "excuse" or simple smoke screen objection, like, "I can't afford it," you need to simply use that as an opportunity to close.

"Oh, you should have said so, we just spread the payments out over time so you can afford it, let’s do this."

“Just go to McDonalds 1 less time per week and this would fit in the budget, you could do that right?”

“Excuse” is another word for justification. Justification is what people do before making any decision. People often don't buy simply because they can't see any convincing self-justification for why they need to make a decision to do it now. There isn't a compelling enough argument, no validation of offering, no company or product, lack of trust, no great need based on price, etc. Show them that you have an amazing product and offering, and then go into this close.

On the Door:

> "Most people don't like to buy from people that come to their door, because when they want something, they go out and buy it. But why everyone works with me today is that I save them X amount of money", or, "is that everyone realizes it is much easier to work with me, and they need it anyway," or, "is that I save them money on something they are already spending money on."
>
> "Don't worry, most people don't buy from people that go door to door, but all these (Bandwagon) people already did what I'm doing, because it was hard to come up with reasons to say no."

In the Home:

> "It sounds like you're coming up with a lot of reasons why this won't work for you, but what you should be doing is listing all of the ways this will benefit you, and then we could make this work. What are some of the main things you like about all of this?"
>
> "It is much easier to talk yourself out of getting something, than to talk yourself into

it, but if we list all of the aspects of this you will like, and then weigh it out with the costs, there won't be any reason in the world you wouldn't do it, I promise."

Bonus Close

Email Close

After going through the deal, simply put your head down and ask them the best email for them.

“So, it comes to about a buck a day, what was the best email for you?”

“I just need to get this info all to you so you have it, what was the best email for you?”

“We do everything electronic, what was the best email for you?”

Exercise:

Write out ways you can flip those excuses into reasons for them to buy?

Feel Felt Found Close

"**I** understand how you feel, **so-and-so** felt the same way, but what **they** found was _____."

USE THIS OFTEN! This is commonly used to overcome an objection. Usually, the best time to close is right after you overcome their concern and then check to see if they are now ready to move forward. This close is really powerful, and helps attack from a 3rd party, not straight on. You can utilize stories within this close as well. Your "Found" can be drawn out as short or as long as you want. This close can be used on the doors or in the home.

The FEEL: "**I** understand how you FEEL."

This is powerful, because you agree with the customer, and validate their feelings. Our natural tendency in sales is to contradict or get defensive with customers. The first rule in sales is **always to agree** with the customer. Sometimes this is hard, because the customer says something ridiculous or something that doesn't make sense. Be humble, and really empathize with them. The easiest way to empathize is just to realize that you have presented the product 1000 times, but this is the first time that they are learning about it. You have studied the ins and outs, and already have a conviction of it, but they don't. This is likely the first time that they have been through your presentation, and more often than not, they aren't going to retain all of things you talk about in your presentation.

When we sense danger, our brains go into a natural survivor mode of either **fight or flight**. The amygdala in the brain tells the endocrine system to release certain hormones, such as cortisol, or adrenaline, that make us shut down, experience shortness of breath, tense up, retreat, and want to either run away or get defensive. The decision-making process creates a fear that comes from losing money, past bad decisions, commitment etc. The fastest way to calm the nervous system of your customer is validation. Simply by saying, "I get you, I feel you, I get how that may feel, you probably get anxious in situations like this, it is totally normal..." If you are married, you understand the power of these words 😉. These phrases release hormones such as serotonin, oxytocin. These two hormones create a sense of certainty, peace, calming, and connection. You want your customers to feel safe with you, not in the "fight or flight" mode.

The FELT: "**Your neighbors** FELT the same way."

You can substitute neighbors with:

- Name of someone they know
- Important figure

- Random name that has a story that relates to their objection

The most powerful name to put here is someone they know. The second that you can connect them with someone credible in the same situation, with the same objections, you will find it will work wonders in your sales.

What the "FELT" does is show that they aren't the only ones that have that concern. Most people think that they are so creative when they come up with an objection, but little do they know you have probably heard every objection in the book 1000 times, and they are just like the rest of the people you meet with. When they realize that they aren't the only ones with that concern, and that it is totally normal to have concerns, they will lighten up. Some people get nervous even bringing up concerns. They feel as if it is offensive to let you know they have a concern. When you show that others have felt the same way, it shows that even though they had concerns, they still moved forward. The customer's truth will start to naturally flow out, creating a positive buying situation.

The FOUND: "What **your neighbors** FOUND was_____."

This is where you solve the problem. You show the customer that after consideration of the concern, their friend realized that it wasn't anything that really got in the way of them buying. Concerns are totally normal, and it isn't anything that you can't work through. You can show them that you are the professional, and that you can walk them through their journey of making a decision because you have done that with tons of others just like them.

Transition:

Transitioning is one of the most powerful pieces in your sales. It is critical after you explain the “Found,” that you MOVE ON. Most rookies common mistake is to pause at this point and wait for a response from the customer to see if their Feel, Felt, Found worked. This is difference between presenters and closers. A close is when you hit them with the close, and then you move on, assuming that you were able to overcome their objection and keep progressing the sale forward. They will bring up a concern again if it hasn't been resolved. Fear of rejection will hold a rep back from pushing for the close. We naturally don't want to hear a "no," so we shy away from pushing the sale along. This is a common mistake found amongst salesman.

Exercise:

Write 3 ways you can incorporate the Feel, Felt, Found Close into your presentation when someone gives you an objection.

Customer Objection 1:

____

____

I understand how you feel, _________________ felt the same way, but what they found was….

____

____

____

____

____

____

____

____

____

Customer Objection 2:

I understand how you feel, ________________ felt the same way, but what they found was....

Customer Objection 3:

____

____

I understand how you feel, _______________
felt the same way, but what they found was

____

____

____

____

____

____

____

____

____

____

____

____

____

....

____

____

____

____

G

Gratitude Close

Showing gratitude and appreciation for your customer 's time. Mention that you truly love working with people like them, and then ask for the sale.

Ask your customer to express what they appreciate about the product, and then ask for the sale.

“Thank You” cards: these can be used as a way to follow-up with your customers, to get referrals, or to ask for the sale a second time.

When you show your customers appreciation, they experience “feel-good” emotions. Everyone likes to feel appreciated, plus it creates a deeper sense of connection to you. Gratitude is the fastest way to change someone's attitude. Often, people feel pressured in a sale, or develop sales resistance. Those feelings are uneasy, which makes it extremely difficult to ask for a sale when they are stirring. We must first help to shift their emotions into something more positive. Then it is much easier to close. Try getting mad at someone who is just yakking on about all of the things they love about you – it is virtually impossible. Emotions can shift in a matter of seconds, and as sales reps, we have the power to achieve that with our customers.

1) Show that you appreciate their time, and how they showed up for you so far in the sale, and the fact that they were open with their concerns and asked great questions.

This will make it much harder for them to say no to you when you ask for the sale. People struggle with rejecting people that they like and feel connected to. If they don't feel this, they will push you away much faster.

2) Ask them to recap what the main things they love about the product or service are.

This will help them to remember the right emotions, versus the wrong emotions, in your sales process. Usually, in the middle of the sale, when you are explaining benefits, people's emotions are positive. But when you start bringing up the price or after paperwork, that can all change.

3) Thank You Cards: these can be an extremely powerful tool in direct selling. When you can personalize a note to someone to show appreciation about specific things in their lives and from the presentation, it can go a long way. Most people don't take the time to do this, but it can pay back tenfold if done right. Most customers have never experienced a salesperson that has gotten authentic with them, and gone the extra mile to send a personalized, handwritten thank you card. Don't just write the card and say thank you,

make sure to go deeper than that. For example:

I wanted to express how grateful I am for the time you took to listen to what I had to say. Most people reject strangers that come to their door, but you took the time to invite me into your home, and listen to what all I had to say. That shows a ton about your character, and your openness to new ideas, and concepts. I really loved seeing how well you parent and interact with your children. You can tell that you really have a strong passion for parenting. I thank you for supporting my cause to really make a difference in as many of your neighbors lives, and bringing a better service into their homes. I am one more deal closer to hitting my goal, and that means a ton that you cared about my own personal goals, and I hope to stay in touch and keep you posted along my journey and success. I wish the best to you and your family.

A thank you card can also be used for people you didn't close. Make sure to be authentic about it, and not come off as a smart ass. This will really bring some power to you, and possibly even make them reconsider their decision. You would be surprised how far that card will go – in six months, they may have a need for your product or service, and call you back. You will stand out to them, versus the other sales guys that are always at their door.

Additionally, Thank You cards can be used to get massive amounts of referrals. Make sure to follow up with customers after they have been using your product for some time, and ask for referrals again. Thank You cards act as a soft touch that makes a difference, so they are warmed up to you when you call or revisit, and ask for more referrals or upsell them. The crazy part about our job is that we focus so much on the next door, that we fail to do a traditional style of effectively selling and mining our current prospects, or working a pipeline properly. We just move through one area, and then on to the next.

Listen to the podcast by John Israel:
"Mr. Thank You."

Soundcloud.com/d2d-podcast

Exercise:

Post on mrthankyou.com that you did it, and support the cause of raising the level of gratitude on this planet by 1%.

Write out 3 good questions that you can ask your client to put them in a state of appreciation.

1.) ____
____
____

2.) ____
____
____

3.) ____
____
____
____

Write 3 Thank You cards to your most current customers.

1) __________________________

2) __________________________

3) __________________________

Bonus Close

Give and Take Close - (Similar to the Win-Win Close page 207)

- If you can ____, I will drop your price to___.
- If you qualify and do ___, I will throw in an extra ___.
- In order for me to give another ____, you have to ____.

High-Five Close

Stating a point that you want them to agree with, and then with confidence giving them a "High-Five."

To some, this may seem very silly, but there is a lot of power behind a high-five or fist bump. According to *The Five Love Languages*, by Gary Chapman, there are five ways to express and experience love:

- Words of Affirmation
- Quality Time
- Receiving Gifts
- Acts of Service
- Physical Touch

You should be using all 5 love languages with your customers throughout the sale, including physical touch. (When you get more advanced, you will be able to pick up on which ones they prefer more than others.) Now, most salesmen aren't going to go in for a hug at the door, or touch someone's leg. But one simple way to implement physical touch is through a high-five. Touch in a sale shows that you are confident, and feel close enough to touch one another. A good shoulder grab goes a long way in the right situation. A high-five is friendlier than a handshake – less business-y and more personal. I have even used fist bumps to close numerous deals, believe it or not. When you can get someone to give you a high-five, it acts just like getting a little “Yes!” moving you closer to the sale. High-fives are even more powerful than a simple yes, and they create a stronger sense of adherence or agreement.

When someone raises their hand to give you a high-five, your mind has been automatically conditioned for your entire life to stick your hand up as well, and follow along. By doing this, you are leading the subconscious mind to agree with you. There are plenty of times that the customer is not nearly ready to agree with you, but they still instinctively react to your request for a high-five. This is a simple way to loosen the customer up, and test their temperature. If a customer resists the high-five, you know right away that they are still ice cold, and you still have some warming up to do.

A high-five is most effective when you are trying to get someone to agree with you on a certain point. They are also commonly used to celebrate wins in a sale. Think about the hormonal release you get when someone gives you a high-five or a "Good job." It is like a shot of dopamine. Dopamine is the hormone that makes your pre-frontal cortex work more efficiently. It helps you make faster and smarter decisions, by connecting your synapses together at a faster rate, and making it easier to process things. This is the “feel good” hormone.

Give your customers small shots of dopamine during the sale, and they will start to feel more confident throughout the presentation. This will make the overall process much smoother, and will make it easier when the time comes for you to get final signatures and payment.

Some of you might be thinking, "It’s only a freaking high-five, for crying out loud,” but the fact of the matter is that everything you do and say in your sales has purpose. Top performers calculate their moves, their body language, their questions, etc. They know what reactions they get from customers when they do certain things. They know how to alter someone's moods, change their thought patterns, and redirect, control and shift the direction of conversation.

"Check this out, you can save $500 a year." (High-five)

"The best part is that it isn't going to cost you anything upfront.” (High-five)

"You're helping the planet, saving money, and I make money, and that's a win-win-win!" (High-five)

"If I can take care of your first month, and you start paying next month, would that be a win? Deal!" (Fist bump)

"Check this out, you're in the business of saving money, right?" (High-five)

"I'll be in and out in less than 10 minutes. Deal?" (High-five)

"You like the sound of that, right?" (Fist bump)

As you can see, this can be used in many different places throughout your pitch, and when used right, creates engagement and connection. It makes things fun and produces a higher energy. It also shows confidence, and brings light-heartedness to the whole situation.

High-fives can also be used as a pattern break. Most customers aren't expecting to get a high-five from some random person at their door. Pattern interrupts are used to throw off their current thought process, and make them think of something new.

For example:

Customer: "Just get to the point and tell me how much this is going to cost me."

Rep: Pattern Interrupt: "That is my favorite part of all of this, I'll make sure I get to that soon. (High-five) But really quick, as I was saying..."

Exercise:

Write down 3 places in your sale that would make sense to give a customer a "HIGH-FIVE."

1.) ____

2.) ____

3.) ____

Bonus Close

Hot Button Close

- 90% of people's buying decisions have to do with 10% of the actual features of your product or service.

Ask, Ask, Ask, Don't Tell, Tell, Tell. It is extremely important to ask as many questions as possible. This strategy is called the "Freudian Slip." What that means is that if you ask enough questions, eventually the customer will tell you all of the things they like about what you're offering. Initially, they aren't going to come right out of the gate letting you know all of their hot buttons. But once you know why they would buy, or what they like most about it, then hammer on that. Coupled well with the Why Close on page 207.

Customer: "Well, I'm not sure if I can afford it."

Rep: "Like you said, having your kids come home from school and being able to check in on them would be priceless."

Customer: "But I still need to shop around."

Rep: "Checking in with the kids from your phone every day."

ETC...

You just keep rehashing their hot button, and eventually they will stop their complaints.

I

Intelligence Close

Utilizing names and stories of influential, highly intelligent people that have bought, in order to bring validity to the sale.

I'm going to lay this out simply, you, kind of want them to feel like an idiot for not buying, or for having a certain concern, due to the fact that intelligent and educated people – doctors, engineers, scientists, policeman, mayors, financial planners, professors, etc. – already had those same concerns and conducted research, but still moved ahead with your product. The best way to use this is to connect them with someone they admire, or look up to in their area, and that they can relate to. Why do you think influencer marketing is so big?

Most people are sheep, and they follow the shepherds (leaders and influencers in our society).

Your job is to position yourself as an influencer by association to other powerful influencers in your potential client's network. You can also just position yourself as the messenger for the influencers. When they see that you have influence, and know more about everything than they do, you gain authority in the sale. Most customers have the tendency to believe they know more about the service or product that you're pitching. They have a need to be right, and to prove you wrong, because it is natural for them to get defensive. When they come to the realization that you actually know what you're talking about, and that others that are very influential also back you, they soften the walls, trust you, and start to open up and listen.

There is a right and a wrong way to use this close. You never want to directly make someone feel stupid. You can indirectly, in a passive way, accomplish this, but it doesn't really invoke good feelings, so you must be careful with how you use it. A common way to soften the blow is by using validation. When customers start to object to you, or take jabs at your product, that is a great time to utilize this.

For example:

> Customer: "This doesn't make sense, because I won't get the return on my investment for like 10 years."
>
> Rep: "That is exactly how most people think, and initially view this before I walk them through it (validation, agree). But after Jerry Smith – he has been in financial planning for the last 25 years, and lives just right behind you, do you know him? He is the one with the blue truck and the big palm trees out front. Well, he picked this apart, and put all of these spreadsheets together. Stuff I really didn't even understand. And after lots of research and talking it over with his accountant, he found that this was an absolute no-brainer, and the breakeven was day 1. He was probably the most skeptical guy I've ever dealt with, but now he recommends me to most of his clients."

You can see that I validated, then I smashed the concern by using a financial planner, and an accountant. My current customer is probably some school teacher trying to act smart, as if they know something about ROI's. I do know how the ROI works, but coming from me it means nothing, considering that I am the sales guy. But coming from the smart neighbor right behind them it carries 10x the weight. Always have an arsenal of these in your back pocket. Keep track of these stories, and use them throughout your presentation. You can do this close even before customers bring up objections.

It is always important after using this close to transition on to the next thing. Below are some good transitions after a close like this:

> "So, the next thing is..."
>
> "Does that make sense?"
>
> "You can see why he said that, right?"
>
> "He probably knows much more than the both of us combined about finance, right?"
>
> "So, what other questions do you have?"

Exercise:

Write out all of the people you have sold that have authority, and how you can use them through your presentations. Quick note on why you would leverage their name in a deal.

NAME	STORY/OBJECTION/AUTHORITY

Bonus Closes

If - Then Close

- Using an If _____, Then _________ statement. Coupled well with the Win- Win Close.

"If I can do ____, then would there be any reason you wouldn't do this today?"

"If you only had to pay ___, then would there be any reason you wouldn't do it?"

"If I could have this installed before your trip, then would you do it?"

Invitation Close

- Simply inviting the customer to move forward and buy.

This may seem basic, but like I've talked about before, people often forget to ask for the order.

"Why don't you try it out?" "Why don't you buy it?"

"How many do you want?"

"When do you want to get started?"

"Would you like us to get rolling on this right away?"

Instant Reverse Close

- If you get an objection, you would simply say:

Rep: "MR. PROSPECT, THAT'S EXACTLY WHY YOU SHOULD TAKE IT."

Customer: "Why do you say that?"

Rep: "You want to get this for the best price? And the best product quality, right? And you're going to buy a system eventually, aren't you? Well, that's exactly why you should take it today at this price, because you won't get a better combination of product, quality, and price as of right now. Why don't you take it?"

Just Do It Close

With confidence, stating, “Just Do It.”

For those that are familiar with NLP (Neuro Linguistic Programing), in sales there is a lot of power in what we call "Embedded Commands." An embedded command is basically like a subliminal message that softly speaks to your client's unconscious mind. Motivational speakers, leaders, coaches, magicians, and salespeople use these frequently, because they have a powerful effect on communication and persuasion. When used for the good, and done right, they can be very effective. The Just Do It Close is a simple embedded command that I have found to be extremely successful. I would recommend studying NLP, as it could be a powerful tool to use throughout your sales and communications. In this book, I won't touch on it much, but in D2Duniversity you will be able to find other courses on it.

This close can be used in the third-person, past tense, or in the command form. Here are a couple of examples:

"The Johnsons down the street were tight on money, and didn't have all the answers, but they JUST DID IT anyway because they liked me, and I gave them such a good deal."

> "Most people JUST DO IT because they realize it's a good deal."
>
> "The price is right, the product is right, and you now know we're a good company, let's JUST DO IT."
>
> "I get that you're not 100% there, but let's JUST DO IT, and if you don't like it, call me and we can refund you."
>
> "You're going to get this eventually, so let's JUST DO IT now."
>
> "Tiffany down the street thought the same thing, but she JUST DID IT anyway."
>
> "I've answered all your questions, right? OK, LET'S DO THIS."

Statements like these need to be said with confidence. If you have doubt in your tone, you lose. Make sure to speak from a place of authority, and be certain that you have done a good job at building the value in your product or service. None of these closes really have any weight if you don't show the value in your product. Confidence is contagious. Most people have a low sense of confidence, and are always unsure about the decisions they make in life. Realize that this is probably how your customer feels. When you can show confidence in what you're doing, and they truly sense that, they will find it much easier to act on what you're pitching.

The Just Do It Close can also be used as a bullying tactic. Not in a bad way, but you can use it to comically, or lightly, put some pressure on a customer.

> Customer: "Sam, I'm not sure if I should do this or not."
>
> Rep: "Just do it." (Make sure to use more of a command tone here.)
>
> Customer: "I know, but what if I move, or lose my job?"
>
> Rep: "There are always 'what ifs'... Just do it, you'll love it." ETC...

Realize that some customers just need an extra push to move forward. People need some validation from a "friend" that they are making the right choices. If you have built the right amount of rapport throughout your sale, you can turn from salesman to friend. You can take away the fear of a wrong choice by comforting them and giving some encouragement through their decision process. Think of a kid trying to jump off the high dive. You might be at the side of the pool yelling, "You got this, just do it, you're not going to die, it's awesome, just do it, c'mon..." This close can be used in a similar fashion.

Exercise:

With confidence, out loud, say and/or write 3-4 different scenarios where you could say, “JUST DO IT!” in your sale.

Knocked on Your Door Close

Explaining that you came to them to do business, and not that they came to you to shop.

"I know you didn't come to me. I knocked on your door. It wasn't like you were sitting on the couch waiting for the Pest guy__ to show up. But at the end of the day, I wouldn't be wasting your time or mine if I didn't have something legit."

"I knocked on your door to earn your business, which is much different from you calling up some call center or going online to buy something. Because typically when you want something, you just do that. I have to make it worth your while to even hear me out."

"If you called into some company, don't you think them just taking your order would be much more expensive, as opposed to me coming to earn your business?"

“I wouldn’t be out here wasting your time or mine unless I had something legit.”

"I knocked on your door to do business today, not to drop off flyers and hand out cards. They usually send out the high school football team to drop off those door hangers, and where do those usually end up? The trash, right? Our program is a little different"

"Its 2017, I know that you're busy and that you weren't waiting for someone to come knocking on your door, but I will make this super quick and worth your time."

"I knock on doors and move around areas quite a bit, if I came back to every customer that asked me to, and left my card, I would be driving literally 100 miles a day. You could understand that, right? I choose not to do that, and I just get these done as I go."

These are just a few examples of how you can use the Knocked on Your Door Close. The concept of this is to leverage the fact that you are knocking, and have a tough job. You respect their time, but you also respect yours. People often don't realize that you walk around a ton and are always on the move. For you to go to some call back in an area that you visited a month ago, it would literally take half of your day. If you use that half a day to just knock where you're knocking, chances are you will sell one just as easily. Top closers who have the mentality of no fear of loss will always close more deals. “Don't be the needy, be the needed,” Ian Wendt in the D2D-Podcast goes into this principle more in depth on maintaining control throughout your sales process.

You have to let them into your world, and set some good expectations upfront. Realize that with all of these examples, I have zero attachment, and I show that I'm fully there to serve them. I also have an abundant mentality when closing. Make sure that you show them that you aren't desperate, and that you have plenty of business. People like to buy when they know that others are buying as well. Naturally, people have a tendency to feel that they can bully salesman, and take advantage of them and their time. This pattern comes from the thousands of BAD salespeople out there who come across as extremely desperate, dote on every customer, and kiss the ground they walk on.

Exercise:

Write out how you can be more abundant in selling and not so need.

L

Last Chance Close

Creating a genuine, positive sense of urgency by giving them one last chance to buy.

The last chance close is designed to create urgency, and to show them that they can't get the same price, or offering, anywhere else, or at any other time. This couples really well with the Knocked on Your Door Close page 119. You can use the Last Chance Close at any point in your sale, but it is most effective if you use it before any major objections come up. It isn't very effective to back peddle and try to get them to buy after they have already told you they don't want to buy today. “8 mile” with this close!

Urgency is such a sensitive subject in selling. No one likes callbacks – everyone knows that if you don't close on your first visit, the likelihood of them buying drops tremendously. Because these are the cold hard facts, use them to your advantage. Urgency is delicate. There is a fine line between a pushy sales person, and one that is crafty in how they create urgency. Sales professionals can create situations that passively push customers into a buying scenario. Most customers resist urgency because they get uncomfortable. As a good salesman, you should learn the power of push and pull. Just like the balloon above – if you were to blow it up really fast, it would pop, and you wouldn't get much out of it. But if you were to stretch the balloon before blowing it up, then blow it up a little, deflate it a little, then stretch it some more, and repeat, you would get much more size and strength out the balloon. When pushing, you should always know when and where to put in some pullbacks.

Pullbacks

Pullbacks are lines that relieve tension. They are lines that show that you aren't desperate (see Qualifying Close page 159). They are lines that put some certainty and calmness back in the customer. A few great one liners that I use are:

> "If you do it, great. If not... not a big deal."

> "At the end of the day, you don't have to buy this."

> "Honestly, you can tell me NO if you don't want it."

> "If it isn't a win-win, then let's not do this."

> "If it makes sense, do it. If it doesn't, don't do it."

> "I'm just leaving you some info, and info doesn't hurt."

> "I don't even know yet if you qualify, so let's not get too far ahead of ourselves."

Urgency and pressure are not bad things. If it weren't for pressure, no one would ever buy, and nothing would ever happen in this world. It is our job to make transactions happen, not to be awesome educators. Many reps fall into the trap of being great presenters, but terrible closers. I hate to break it to you, but if you fall into that category, it is on you, not on your customers, product, or area. Guess what – your company probably wouldn't exist if someone wasn't selling lights out in the same type of area, with the same type of customers.

You have to learn what they are doing to CLOSE!

Examples of the Last Chance Close:

"They sent me out here to get the initial few people on the promotional rate, so that we can get future business by people being more familiar with the company and product later on."

"For those that work with me today, I pay for ____. For those that want to call in later, I gladly give them the 1-800 number, and they can get it at normal price."

"Today only, we waive the ____, because we're doing this competition to get another 10 people by the end of the day, and my boss is really pushing for that."

"You can get this anytime you want, but if you go with me now, I will take care of your__. But if this is going to be some drawn out, back and forth thing, then let's just not do it at all."

"We only have 3 spots left on the route for this week. If we can get you on our route, and knock them all out at the same time, we will discount the price by ___.

"The reason that I can pay for your install is because we already have our techs out here today."

Bonus Close

Last Name Close

After working out the financial details simply ask: "What is the exact spelling of your last name?"

By moving on to their name and writing it down it implies you are closing the deal. Most people don't associate the two, and they will willingly give you their name. There is less resistance to this question than just simply asking, "so do you want to do this?"

Exercise:

Write out 3 powerful pullbacks you can use throughout your sales process.

1.) ____
____

2.) ____
____

3.) ____
____

Write out 3 ways you can create urgency in your sales process without bringing too much unwanted pressure on the customer, and without coming off as gimmicky.

1.) ____
____

2.) ____
____

3.) ____
____

M

Manager Call Close

When someone is asking for a better deal, you don't just give it to them, you get approval from above so that they feel special.

When a customer is trying to milk you for a special deal, instead of just giving in and giving it to them, fight it for a minute, and then call your "manager" to get it approved. People always feel special if you make a call to a superior to help them out.

Customer: “I honestly just think this is too steep.”

Rep: “Hypothetically, if I call my manager and he approves of me taking $10 off per month, would you do it?”

OR

“I can’t do anything more for you, but let me call my manager, and see what else he may be able to do. If he can give you a little better of a deal, I wouldn’t be wasting my time, right? He doesn’t like me calling him all the time.”

Customer: “Yeah.”

Rep: “I'm not making any promises, because they don't normally do this. And I have basically been tapped out trying to discount these, so my manager gets kind of mad at me. But if you make the rest of this process go smooth, and we can get this done quickly, then I'll call him."

Customer: "Sounds good."

Rep: (Calls manager) "Hey John, I'm here with the Johnsons, and they are the nicest family, they have a ton of connections in this neighborhood, and they told me they would give me a few references if I could lower their bill by $10. I know I have asked you a few times on this, and that you told me to stop calling you because you get in trouble, but would it be too much to ask to get these guys that deal?"

Rep: (To customer) "He basically, said that I could do it under the condition that you give me a couple of names that I can go to after this appointment. They don't have to buy, but that is what would make it worth it to him, and me, to do this for you. Would that work?"

Customer: "Yeah, we know some people." (indicates a yes)

Rep: "Perfect, let's do this..." (Transition)

This close is super effective when you have a strong negotiator. Make sure to build up your manager before you call them, so that your customer sees them as extremely high up in the company, and very well taken care of, versus just the peon that goes door to door. Even as the VP of a company, I have still used this close, and called one of my reps. They know when I start the conversation with, "Hey, I'm here with a customer...," that they will play the manager. Most of the time I already know what pricing deals I can and can't do, but it still has more weight coming from someone else.

This is very well coupled with the Discount Close or the Competition Close (page 59). Make sure that the manager is also trained on this close. It will help direct the conversation in a more positive way. The customer will feel more special, and who doesn't like to feel special?

Remember the give and take rule. My favorite thing to ask of the customer is for referrals, and for them to connect me to them. If you listen to the D2D-Podcast "10 Step Referral Process," it will really teach you a great systematic way to get way more referrals.

Exercise:

Who are the 3 people that you are going to communicate with to let them know that you may call them to do that manager call?

1) ______________________________
2) ______________________________
3) ______________________________

What discount can you have prepared to ask your manager for that will make an ideal win-win scenario for the customer?

____
____
____
____
____
____
____
____
____
____
____

N

Not Interested Close

Used when a customer keeps bringing up that they are "not interested." Can be used at the door or in the home.

If you are sick of hearing the words NOT INTERESTED, make sure to read this. The Not Interested Close is designed to “8 Mile” someone you sense isn't really following you, or isn’t interested/engaged, or as a rebuttal to the phrase "not interested."

> "I know this isn't something you have ever been interested in, because if you were, you would already have it."

> "Money isn't the issue. It seems it really is just the fact that you never saw the need for this, right? Because if you did, you would already have it."

> "Most people aren't super interested in this until after they need it. But once they need it, it’s too late. We take more of a proactive approach and help people get this before the fact, instead of after the fact."

> "Most people are reactive and procrastinate. Let’s be real, this isn't something that has been on the top of your list, and isn’t a super FUN buy. But at the end of the day, I'm

here now, and I make it cheap and simple for you to finally get this done."

"Most people have been hit up by other people coming to the door about this, and they always say the same thing..."I'm not interested." That is what you told the last few guys, right? Perfect, because I'm doing something totally different..."

"I know this isn't something you typically would go out and shop for, so that is why I'm here. It's because if it weren't for people like me, most people would never benefit from what we do. I got you." (High-Five Close)

"There isn't a (home service) store in town you can just walk in and get this, how else do you think people go about getting these types of things? I mean you have to talk to someone like me..."

These are just a couple of examples of lines you can use to “8 mile,” or rebuttal "not interested." Never see this as a real objection.

There are 3 types of objections: Smoke Screen, Real Objection, and Conditions.

Smoke Screens are when people just say whatever comes to their head first to get you to go away, or to try and regain control of the situation. These should be brushed off or ignored. Too often reps will try and spend time on smoke screen objections as if they are a true concern, which actually puts the customer in control, and will derail your sales process.

Real Objections are when a customer actually has a concern or obstacle they are facing that needs to be addressed before they are ready to buy. These should be validated and dealt with before trying to ask for the sale.

Conditions are things that stop customers from being able to buy. Failed credit, renter, job loss or moving. They are things outside your control that will never be overcome. Don’t waste your time with customers that have a condition that makes it impossible for you to sell. Also, don’t get discouraged when facing conditions, it is just part of the job.

Objections should be heard as questions, meaning that when someone says, "Not interested," you should hear, "Tell me more about why I should be interested in this."

"I can't afford this," turns into, "Show me how I can afford this today".

"I don't have time," turns into, "Show me quickly how this is worth my time to listen to."

"Already have one," turns into, "Show me how you are 10x better and are worth the hassle of switching."

“Another company stopped by already,” turns into, “Tell me why you are better than the last guys I told no to.”

You get the picture, right? Too often, reps get discouraged way too fast from objections, and the fact of the matter is that they take it way too personally. They are hearing them the wrong way. Train your brain to take objections much lighter, and it will help you to maintain a much more positive attitude throughout the day, and to have more confidence.

When two people meet, the person with the most confidence wins. The Not Interested Close is only effective when you show utter confidence and control of the sale. If you come off at all timid with your body language, or seem unsure of yourself, this close won't work. Closing is a transfer of enthusiasm. People can sense more of your essence than you realize. If you give off the aura of a badass, then people respect that. They tend to walk all over the weak. When reps get beat up no matter what neighborhood they go to, it is usually a reflection of how they are showing up in their essence. They are being weak and timid in their approach, and this makes them a much easier target for people to pick on. It is hard to pick on someone that is sure of themselves, confident, and full of energy and authority. This is probably one of the main differentiators between top performers and lower performing reps.

Exercise:

Write down the 5 most common objections you are getting, and how you should now hear them.

1.) ______________________________

____

____

____

2.) ______________________________

____

____

____

3.) ______________________________

____

____

____

4.) ______________________________

____

____

____

5.) ______________________________

____

____

____

Write out how you can "8 Mile" the objection "not interested" at the **door**.

Option Close

Giving people options to pick from so that they are the ones making a decision, resulting in a YES or YES scenario.

"People like to buy, they don't like to be sold."-- Brian Tracy.

This is one of the most powerful closes, and can be used in many ways – from setting appointments, to picking products or packages, to closing the deal. The power behind it is that it is taking the back seat, and giving the customer the power to drive.

If we funnel people down to two simple options, it is easier for their brains to process, and makes it more comfortable for them to make a decision. A common pitfall of selling is bombarding the customer with too many options. They will then get overwhelmed, and almost every time they will want to "Think about it" – the three deadliest words in sales. Our brains can only process so many bits per second, so if you narrow things down to the best two options for them, it makes the decision super easy.

- "Do you want a 12-year finance or a 20-year?"
- "You want the lowest monthly payment or the overall lowest total cost?"

- "Would Tuesday at 3pm or 6pm be better for you?"
- "Would you rather have a glass break or a motion?"
- "You want the premium package or the basic?"

This close is designed to test the temperature of the customer. You must look at your customer as a thermometer. You can gauge this based on how quickly and confidently they respond to your option close.

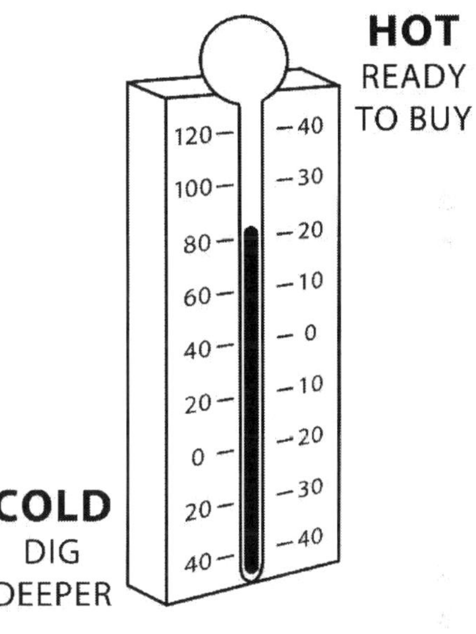

You transition when they are hot. If they are cold, do things to create a fire under them to spark more interest. Ask deeper questions, speak more to their hot buttons, spend more time in discovery to find more interests, or build more trust with the customer.

Exercise:

Write 2 option closes for the product you offer:

1) ______________________________

2) ______________________________

Write 2 option closes that have nothing to do with your product:

1) ______________________________

2) ______________________________

Write 2 option closes that have to do with price:

1) ______________________________

2) ______________________________

Bonus Close

Ownership Close

• Using language as if the customer already bought. (Similar to Assumption Close page 46)

- "Your system will work like this."
- "Your install will happen ___."
- "Your Technician, when he gets here, will put your panel...."
- "Your service will happen 4 times per year..."

Puppy Dog Close

A try it out, or trial close. Having them sign up with the right to cancel within short time frame. Hopefully, once they have it and use it, they will decide to keep it.

This gets its name because when people are selling puppy dogs, they know that if they get the prospect to take the dog home, they will fall in love with it, and it will be extremely hard to take it back. The logic behind this is that you have two options:

1) Customer says let me think about it, and you lower your chances significantly of getting the sale.

2) Customer buys, you get a sale, and have a much higher chance of it sticking than not.

Examples of the Puppy Dog Close:

> "Look, just try it out. You have three business days, and if you don't like it, you can get all of your money back, guaranteed."

> "Would you ever buy a car without test driving it? No? So, this is the same thing. It is hard to make the most educated decision without at least trying it out. If you don't like it, we can come back, and it won't cost you a dime."

"Give us a shot now, and if we don't deliver, then we get you your money back."

"I'll give you one month free, and if in that first month we don't knock your socks off, then cancel. No biggy."

"What if you had a back door, and some time to think about it? Meaning you get it, and there are no strings attached for the next few days, if you feel like I twisted your arm into this. Would you do it?"

"Realistically, how much time do you need to think on this? A few days, or a few weeks? (Answer: a few days). Let's compromise – if I give you a few days to think on it, you have to let me get my portion done today so that I don't have to go back and forth to your home. (Knocked on Your Door Close) Worst case scenario, you cancel in a day or so once you do your homework. Does that sound fair?"

"I'm going to get a 90% yes today so we can at least start the process, if we run into road blacks we can always pause or cancel."

There are thousands of ways you can use this close, but be sure to show that you are confident that once the customer has it, they will love it. You just need them to taste it first.

CANCELS ARE NORMAL! You would be surprised how many times low performing reps come to me and say, "Well I don't have as many cancels as you do."

My response is simple: "You also don't have as many sales as I do."

Reps get in a mindset that cancels are bad. It is just part of sales – accept it now, and deal with it. Cancels sometimes devastate reps, and can ruin them mentally because they aren't prepared for them. Leaders, instill in your reps that cancels are normal, and that they should plan on a certain percentage of deals canceling. Too many reps spend their money before it is truly funded. In some sales jobs, commissions can equal your mortgage payments, and when that deal cancels, you're now up a creek without a paddle because you live sale to sale. This is a terrible habit to get into, so don't put yourself in a position where cancels matter. The more abundant you can be, the more deals you will sell. I will sell anyone and everyone, and if they cancel, they cancel, and I move on. The alternative is to sell far less, still have a few cancels here and there, and make a whole lot less money.

Granted, there are many ways to minimize cancels, and to help make accounts stick, but at the end of the day, you have to control what you can control. Here are a few pointers to help retain your customers after using the Puppy Dog Close.

One powerful way is getting **referrals**. When someone is willing to give you referrals, they are more likely to stick, because they know you will be contacting their network, and it looks bad if the referrer cancels.

Another tip is to **follow up**. Don't be afraid to make contact, stop by, drop off a note, send a text, make a call, etc. within their three days of rescission. Reps sometimes get scared to talk to their customers after they sell them. That is probably a bad sign about your product, your selling style, or how you view yourself. You should be easily able to pick up the phone and call your people and feel confident that they are extremely happy with whatever you sold them. If you're not, switch to a company or product that makes you feel that way.

You can also make sure to **install something** in the home as quickly as possible. Once they have a product in hand, or a service rendered, they are 10x more likely to stick. Make sure your operation creates a way for your service to be delivered as fast as possible.

Make sure to **collect payment**. If you fail to get payment, then there isn't any skin in the game on the customer's end, which makes it even easier for them to cancel, because they don't have to go through a refund process.

Leave them with something special – a card, picture of your family, a unique closing gift, a book, or a thank you note. This ties them to you as a person, rather than them just being tied to the product.

Get **all signatures**. Signatures are a sign of commitment. They don't carry as much weight as payment, but they still have valid meaning. Don't count a sale unless you get all of the proper signatures you need.

Exercise:

Write down 1 way you could Puppy Dog Close someone at the end of your deal.

Bonus Closes

Pros and Cons Close (aka, Ben Franklin Close)

• Having the customer list all of the pros and cons of buying or not buying your service.

Then ask, "Well, do the pros outweigh the cons? If so, let's do this!"

Pen Close

• "Do you have a blue or black pen?"

This is powerful because you are asking them to go get you something, and if they go get a pen, it most likely means signing time. This is a simple way to test the waters. You could also ask for a piece of paper on which to write things down. You could ask for something that means you're ready to do business. For example, in solar, I would use photos of their attic to lock down the deal. If they get up and show me the attic, they will for sure sign. They won't get that far unless they are pretty much committed.

Price Product Company Close

• "Usually, the only reason that someone wouldn't do this right now is because of one of these three things: Can't afford it, don't feel the product is the right fit, or don't know enough about the company to know if they are the right fit. Which one is it?"

If they say none of them, then simply say, "If it is the right product, you can afford it, and you know that we are giving you a good service and company to back it, I just need the best email for you…" Transition, and assume the sale.

Price Drop Close

- Building so much value in what you're offering by listing ALL of the features again, then simply asking, "For all of this, what do you think it would cost you? "If done right, they should say a number much higher than what it is really going to cost them. You would then say, "Yeah, you were close, it is normally right around that." Write down for them a price a little lower than what they tell you, but much higher than what it will eventually be.

This is the perceived value, and that is what people justify buying off of. If they view the real price as being much lower than the perceived value, they are apt to buy.

You then say, "If you can do ___, ___, and ___ for me today, it will only cost X a month. That's it. That's why Tom, and James, and all of your other neighbors did it."

Pick a "P" close, and write it out for your industry

____

____

____

____

____

____

____

____

Qualifying Close

Pulling back to draw the customer further in. Relieve buying pressure by showing uncertainty about whether or not they even qualify for your deal.

"I'm not sure if you qualify yet, so let's start there..."

"Before you and I get ahead of ourselves, the first step is that we should see if you even qualify for this."

"I have a few requirements in order for you to qualify..."

"Not every home is a good fit for this. I ask a series of questions to see if you are even a good candidate."

"How's your credit?"

What you are doing is taking pressure off the sale, and showing that you aren't desperate. See Last Chance Close (page 124). There is a very true sense to qualifying for your offering: credit, roof type, income, contract length, home owner, taxes, and many other things can make or break sales. You can leverage these things to take away the offering.

Often, it is hard to move straight to signing contracts, but it is a much softer transition going into a credit check or something like that.

For example, in solar, a simple one is using the site survey as a "qualification" to see if their roof passes. By doing this, it is easier for them to move the sale along, because they are just seeing if they even qualify.

Once they find out that they qualify, it is easier to then ask for the sale. I like to almost celebrate and make a big deal out of the fact that they are special, and they can now get your service. When someone qualifies, you should now feel 100% certain that they are going to be moving forward, and it should boost your internal energy toward the deal. It should almost be expected that if they went through the whole qualification process, and passed, then they must buy.

Bonus Close

Question Close

- Asking smart, open-ended questions that make the customer answer in a positive way.

  This can be very well coupled with the Qualifying Close, to force them to convince *you* that they are sold enough for you to really hook them up with a good deal.

  I create my own qualifying questions in the sale to help tie down the customer. I want them to sell themselves, not for me have to sell them. Another name for these types of questions is "Tie Downs."

Think of the movie “Gulliver’s Travels,” with Jack Black. In order to trap a giant, you need hundreds of little ropes to tie him down. Same thing in your sale – you must have a lot of little yes's, or experiences where the customer is agreeing with you, and digging themselves deeper and deeper into a hole that is hard for them to jump out of at the end.

Some simple examples of questions that I frequently ask customers, in an organized manner, are:

"Do you consider yourself a vocal person? So, if you liked a product or service, you would recommend it?"

"How often would you use this? Once a year, once a month, once a week, or once a day?"

"When would you see the most savings?"

“What time of year do you see the most bugs?”

"If you were to tell one friend about this, what would you tell them?

"What are the main reasons you would get this?"

"Out of all the things I've shown you so far, what has stood out to you the most?"

These are questions that, in a sense, make the customer agree to buying. These questions will 99% of the time result in positive outcomes, and will help open them up to being closed. Question based selling is the most powerful way to go. Master utilizing questions, and people won't need you to explain every little detail, or talk for an hour. You can end up saying very little, and still get a massive point across, simply because you are chipping away at information that most customers already know, but just don't realize that they know it. A great book on this topic is *Spin Selling*, by Neil Rackham.

Exercise:

What are 5 good questions you can ask your customer in order to make them think, and see value in your product or service?

1) ______________________________

2) ______________________________

3) ______________________________

4) ______________________________

5) ______________________________

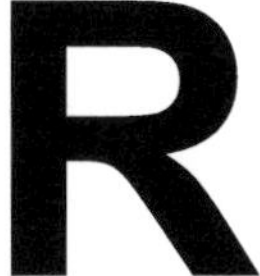

Research Close

Taking the need for research out of the equation for them. Assisting with the research.

At the end of the day, when you leave a customer's home, they aren't going to sit at a computer for hours on end looking up comparisons, call 40 other companies, and read every piece of information out there about your service or product. They may have every intention of doing more research, but what will likely happen instead is that you will leave, they will toss your card away, and will forget about you until the next time you come knocking on their door. Let's just face the facts now, and do something about it.

I start off with a few basic things when they bring up this concern.

"Obviously, I didn't touch on everything fully, and it seems you have a question. I take every question extremely seriously – what questions do you have?"

Think about it – if they didn't get all of their questions answered, and still have more questions that need to be answered, they likely figure they can just find those answers online after you leave. Help with that by showing them that even though it's a lot to take in, you will spend as much time as needed while you're there to make sure that they feel comfortable moving forward. Because at the end of the day, you can find anything on the internet – good or bad – about any company if you look hard enough. The thing you can't find on there is a great, honest, talking salesperson sitting in your living room.

"So, what are some of the main things you want to research?"

"Usually, people look up one of these three things: pricing comparison, similar products/fact check the products being offered, or look into the company they would be going with. Am I in the right ballpark? If so, it's pretty simple. I come prepared, because if you knew you were getting a great deal, with a great product, and that our company was legit, would you do it?"

Great opportunity to close them right there. Then, help walk them through the research, and lock them down!

Jordan Belfort the "Real Wolf of Wall Street" goes into a principle he calls the three "10's of Certainty." If people are not 100% certain on the following 3 things they will not buy.

Customers must be 10 out 10 on your Product, Company, and YOU. If they are a 10 on 2 of those, but only a 6 on the other they will not move forward. Make sure to build trust and certainty on all 3 aspects of your offer. You aren't just selling a product, you are selling your company and yourself.

People these days have smart phones and Google... USE IT! Most of the time, when someone says, "I want to research it," what are they going to do? They are going to put your product or your company in Google, and see what pops up. So why in the world don't you do this for them? Simply pull up the Google search engine, and play to your strengths. Search the keywords that you know are going to show your product or company in a favorable way.

For example, if you have a good BBB rating, but a poor Yelp rating, show how your company has great reviews by searching in Google for "____ company reviews BBB." That will help you to guide the direction of the research for the customer.

> "You probably want to make sure we're a legitimate company and that I'm not just some fly by the night guy, right?"

> "I totally see why you would want to check us out. I mean, what legitimate company knocks on people's doors?! Just kidding! But for real, I know I just showed up from nowhere, and if I were in your shoes, I would look us up too."

I always carry with me my main competitor's bids. If I can save them tons of time and effort going and getting bids, and they trust me, they won't waste their time, and they'll just believe the ones that I show them.

> "I'll give you $100 if you can name me five other (______ i.e. solar, pest, alarm companies) here in (----location----)."

When you put them on the spot like that, they probably only think of 1-2. This brings up the point that they are just going to try to Google more. Have the quotes from the main 1-3 companies that everyone is going to say, and know how to present those quotes against your company to show why they may be good, but that you are a much better option. This will help eliminate the need for them to now go shop around.

Another tactic is using this close with the Puppy Dog Close (page 149).

> "If I gave you a few days, with 0 attachments, to do your homework, would that be enough? Good, so let's compromise. I'm going to get all of my portion done, so I don't have to go back and forth, back and forth (Knocked on Your Door Close page 119), and then if over the next few days you find something that doesn't sit well with you, you can cancel and get all of your money back."

This is powerful mainly because most of the time, people don't take the time to do the research, and they don't want to go through the hassle of canceling

Exercise:

Write out the 3 key things that customers usually want to research at the end of your presentation.

1) ______________________________________
2) ______________________________________
3) ______________________________________

Write out why you think they would want to research those 3 things

____
____
____
____
____
____
____
____
____
____
____
____
____
____
____
____
____

Write out how you are going to "8 Mile" those specific 3 things in your presentation so they don't feel that they need to research them. How can you touch on them so that the customer feels good about them?

____

____

____

____

____

____

____

____

____

____

____

____

____

S

Spouse Close

Utilizing the spouse as an ally to help close the more stubborn spouse or decision maker. Closing with only one spouse there.

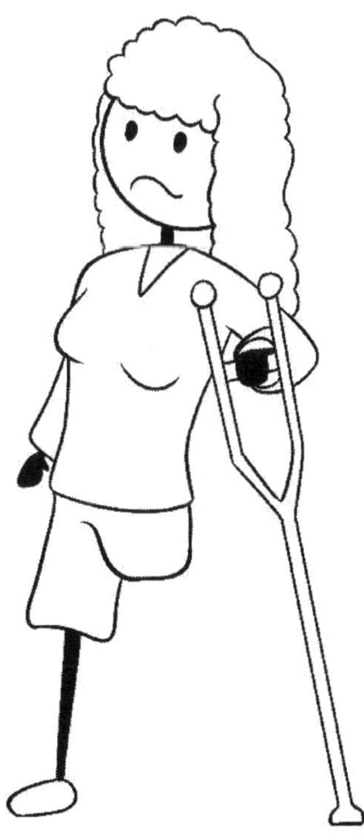

Often, we won't catch both parties present. We need to realize that it is possible for one leg to make decisions, because it happens all the time in their daily lives. Let's face it, every time a wife goes to the mall, she doesn't call her husband before buying the cute pair of jeans she sees. With every bill that comes into their home, they don't really sit down and discuss it, and check their budget to see if they can afford it. Americans get what they want, even if they don't have the money to buy it. That is why most Americans have thousands of dollars on credit cards at any given moment.

Step 1: Identifying who the **decision maker** is in the family.

It is hard to close people if they have very little say in the finances. Sometimes, they both really are the decision makers, and because of that, you can close one or the other. Some cultures simply give little to no power to the wives. Accept and honor that, and don't waste your time. There are a few ways to quickly figure out who you need to be dealing with:

1) Ask:

   - "Who is the one that typically pays the bills and whatnot?"

- "Who's in charge of the finances?"
- "Who wears the pants in the family?"
- "Who's the boss?"
- "Is this something that would be in your department, or your spouses?"

What is extremely funny is that when they answer, "Oh that would be both of us," that personal typically isn't the decision maker. They are just ashamed to admit the fact that their spouse runs the house. Rarely is it the case that both partners have 50/50 weight about where the finances go.

2) Pay attention to how they respond to your questions.

Often, the one that has lesser say in the family will look to the decision maker for validation. The decision maker tends to speak up quickly, and tends to be the tougher sale. You can tell who is who when they seek approval upon listening, or ask certain questions, or respond with very obvious buying signs. Your job is to pitch the decision maker, and make an ally of the lesser of the two.

Step 2: Create Allies

Allies in your sales make a huge difference. I like to use lines like, "Hey, you have to help me work on your husband, tell him ALL the reasons you can think of why this would mean the world for you to have." Get the kids involved – sometimes they have a big influence on the parents when making decisions. You must win over the easy ones fast, so they can help you win over the harder ones.

Never assume who is the decision maker. You can screw up your entire sale by doing this, because you focus on the wrong person the whole time, and neglect the one that really should be getting the majority of your attention.

Step 3: Get both spouses on the same page as often as possible.

Many times, you'll be presenting to the husband while the wife is in the other room taking care of the kids. Sometimes one is already in bed. Do everything possible to drag them both into it. Once you manage to get the other leg there, start over, and rebuild value from the top. Don't assume that she is just going to be on board – they need to be able to put their two cents in. If the present spouse sees that they are involved and participating, it will give them more confidence in deciding. This also takes away the excuse that all people want to use: "Well this all sounds great, I'll just discuss it over with the wife/husband." Take this situation away as much as possible if the spouse is present or easy to access by phone. More often than not, they don't really need to talk to their spouse, because they are the end all say all in the family – they are just using this as an easy cop out to say "no."

Some good lines to draw the other spouse into the presentation are:

> "Look, my company makes me ask you and your spouse a few questions, but they require both to answer, so is it cool if you grab her just for these three questions?" "To save myself, and yourself, a ton of time – because you know just as well as I do that one of us is going to have to repeat this whole thing to your wife anyway – could you go grab her so we can knock two birds out with one stone?"

"Is this something the both of you would decide on? If so, I need to talk to both of you."

"Can you go grab your husband? It's important that he is here."

Step 4: Ask for the Sale

Be direct, and don't be afraid to try these multiple times throughout the sale. Sometimes they won't come the first time, but then try again in a few minutes until they do. Lazy closers don't fight to get the other leg there. Sometimes, if I know that the one I'm talking to isn't the decision maker, I don't waste my time. I leave and set up another time when they are both willing to meet with me.

How to use The Spouse Close:

There are 3 scenarios I'll go over, and how this close would be used differently in each.

1) You are talking to the decision maker, and the other spouse isn't home.

The difference between top performing and low performing reps is that the top producing can sell one-leggers. Many times, reps get in the habit of thinking that the only good time to knock is between the hours of 5-8pm, because that is when you can catch both spouses at home. I've got news for ya'll – if you listen to the top performing reps in the D2D podcasts, you will find that ALL of them get deals before five. Learn to close one-leggers, and you could potentially double your numbers.

> "Hypothetically, if your spouse were here right now, and said, 'Honey, it's up to you,' what would you tell me right now?"
>
> "Just suppose your spouse said yes, where would you be at right now?"

This is either going to bring up another objection, or they will say "Yes." You are just helping them realize that that is what their spouse is going to say anyway.

You also want to eliminate the cop out objections of just pawning off the responsibility to their spouse to make any decisions. I often will tell sales people that my wife makes all the decisions because personally I don't like saying "no" to people.

2) You are talking to the spouses together, and they still say they want to talk about it.

> "I get you guys want to be on the same page, and I know I've been doing a lot of the talking here. So, Spouse 1, what do you think about all of this right now? Spouse 2, what are your thoughts? Knowing that you both are for it, then let's make this happen!"

> "Hey, I get it, you guys probably want some time to go over stuff while I'm not sitting here breathing down your neck. I have a few phone calls and texts that I have to take really quick, so I'll step outside and give you a second to yourselves."

Step outside for around 10 minutes, and make yourself seem busy. You could add a plug like, "We don't really need to overcomplicate things, it really comes down to: do we want it, or do we not want it?"

3) You are talking to the non-decision maker only.

NOTE: YOU CAN CLOSE THESE PEOPLE!

EGO is your best friend. Nobody likes to feel inferior, and you can play to their pride in an effective way in order to get them to buy. You should do things to really try to make them feel like the decision maker. These types of lines are going to help you soften them up for making a decision at the end of the sale. These are just a few things to help empower the non- decision maker:

"If your spouse were right here right now, what do you think he would love most about this?"

> "You know your spouse better than anyone, you tell me what he would like and not like?"
>
> "If your spouse is anything like mine, when I want something, and know it's a good deal, it's ok if I buy it. Because if my spouse did the same, I would support her in her decisions."
>
> "This isn't like buying a new car or house, we're talking ___ a month, nothing crazy."
>
> "You buy things all the time without calling your spouse, right? Or is it something like every time you swipe your card you have to call them?"
>
> "He/She lets you make decisions in the home too, right?"

Exercise:

Who tends to make the decision on purchasing your product? Husband, wife, or both?

Write down the 3 reasons a spouse would not buy without talking to their other half.

1) ______________________________

2) ______________________________

3) ______________________________

Write down why none of that matters.

____

____

____

____

____

____

____

____

____

____

____

____

____

____

Write down a few closes you could use to get the one-legger to buy.

Time Frame Close

Setting expectations on what your time frame consists of to create urgency, and to ensure that the customer has proper expectations.

BE IN CONTROL! When you set the proper time frame for when things are going to happen, it puts you in control of the situation. Clearly walk/talk your customer through the basic steps of your sales process, and you will find that they will just follow them.

"You have to work with me and my time frame, that way I don't have to be the guy that goes back and forth, back and forth, begging you to do this. I just get these done as I go. That’s not a big deal, right?"

"My techs are in the area, so they just get these done as they go"

"How we save so much on costs is by bundling all your neighbors, and knocking them out at the same time. As long as you’re willing to do that, I can get you this price."

"Today, I get the first step of the process done, and then you'll have a site survey– which takes a few weeks, and then we come install. So, it is a process, and my job today is just to get the initial documents signed and to schedule the site survey."

"We are doing your neighbors tomorrow, and if we can get you on that same route, we will discount your system to save us the trip.

"Because your time and my time is extremely valuable, I want to make sure that I get all of your questions answered, and explain everything you need to know to make an educated decision today. Whether that is yes, or no, is up to you. That way, I don't have to be back and forth all over the map"

"It will take about 20 minutes to go over our program – if you have more questions it could last a little longer. At the end of it all, if you're happy with everything, we get things rolling today, and then install usually happens within the week."

"You set the timer for ___ minutes, and if I'm not done by then, and you're not 100% sold on this, kick me out and I'll stop bugging you, fair?"

This close is designed to help set a good expectation for your intentions and for what the timeline looks like. Sometimes people don't realize that the process typically only takes one visit. Sometimes people don't realize that they can make a decision today. Sometimes reps fail to close people simply because they don't set their sell up for a close, and don't ask for the sale. What this close does is side-step the drawn out back and forth sales process, because you let them know that you don't really do business that way. Too often customers believe you're there to just present them and not to do actually close and collect. This close is well coupled with the Knocked on Your Door Close (page 119).

People don't operate very well when they don't really know the direction that you're going. Naturally, we don't like the unknown, and we don't like surprises. As a rep, you can take away all surprises and alleviate the fear of the unknown by using this close. Your job as a closer is to break down all of the potential obstacles that could get in the way of closing a deal.

Expectations

You will find more satisfied customers because the expectations are set up front. One of the most common reasons companies or reps get complaints is because of mismanaged expectations. Reps often over-promise and under-deliver, and that is the fastest way to lose business. For example, in solar, you should tell people that the install typically takes around three months. If it happens sooner than that, great. But if you tell a customer it is going to take one month, and then it takes three, you will have an extremely unhappy customer. Take the opportunity with the Time Frame Close to create the proper expectation from your customer. They don't know any different, so you really have a blank canvas to work off of.

Time Management

Reps forget how valuable their own time is. Every time you spend too long with a customer that isn't buying, it is taking away from a potential sale. Top reps all learn how to shorten the length of their sales. They learn the balance of rapport building, presenting, questions, and firming up the sale. To sell more deals in the day, you can't be dragging your feet in someone's home, loathing the fact you have to get back out on the streets in the beating sun.

Customers also appreciate when you make sales happen in a timely manner. If someone knocked on my door unexpectedly, and then took 3 hours of my night, I would get fairly upset as well. Make sure that you guide the sale along quickly and efficiently. Be mindful when you go off on tangents, and when you are running in circles. Look for things to cut out of your presentation that don't carry much weight.

Reps also get complacent after one or two sales, and start to slow things down. They lose their sense of urgency. Make sure to stay hungry all the way till the end of the day. By operating this way, you will be surprised how many more deals you will sell.

Exercise:

Write out the steps to your sales process.

1) ______________________________
2) ______________________________
3) ______________________________
4) ______________________________
5) ______________________________
6) ______________________________

Write down how you are going to use the Time Frame Close with your customers.

WHAT IS YOUR TIME WORTH?

Write down how much money you want to make this year. ______________________________

Write down how many hours per week you're committed to working in order to make that much money.

____

____

Write down how many weeks you are going to take a vacation from knocking. ______________

Take $________ Earned / (Hours ___________x (52-Weeks off _______)) =

Hourly Rate: ________________________

Now ask yourself – is your time better spent chasing a customer that is going to drag you around, hanging by a thread, just to possibly tell you no down the road, or is it better to take some time to go knock on another door that is fresh, and has a much higher chance of closing? Knowing what your hourly rate is, do you really want to waste time?

Commit to selling with an abundant mindset – where you are not the one in need, you are the needed!

Upsell Drop Price Close

Shooting for the biggest package possible, then dropping the price from there based on the package that best fits the customer.

Giving value to every benefit or feature, and then giving it away for free or at an extreme discount. The Stack.

Great when coupled with the Zero Down Close (page 222)

Method 1: Shoot for the big kahuna sale, then lower packages until the customer at least buys something.

You never know who is going to buy the biggest package, or who will bite with the most expensive price. It is much easier to start high and then come down, than it is to show your lowest costs, and then keep adding to it. People would always rather see prices go down than up.

Step 1) Show them all that your company has to offer, and really sell them on as many benefits as possible.

Step 2) Try to close on that package. - Customers doesn't bite.

Step 3) Ask, "So out of all the things I've shown you, what are the things that you like the most?"

Step 4) Ask, "Based on your budget what are you open to spending today?" "If you could design the perfect package, what would that look like?"

Step 5) Start taking things off, and then re-close.

-Repeat until customer finally caves and gets something.

The best example of this is Cutco Knives. They have a Haymaker set that costs around $3000. That is what would garner the best commission, and is the biggest set. They don't get a customer to spend $3000 on cutlery every time, but they may leave with a few knives sold for a $200 value. A deal is a deal, but if they never brought up the Haymaker, they would never sell it. You also never know if they enjoyed that knife so much that in six months they call you back and end up buying the whole set.

Method 2: The Stack

If you only pay attention to one piece of this entire book, this should be it. I questioned giving you 100% of the answers for mastering closing, but then felt like if I didn't lay out everything for you, I would be doing ya'll a disservice. HINT: THIS IS EXACTLY WHAT I DO! And I have sold MILLIONS of dollars door to door.

This is used when really trying to demonstrate value. Every piece of your offering has some sense of value. Your company may not even put a price to it, but it isn't a bad option for you to put a dollar value to certain things in your sale. For example, in solar, we offer a manufacture panel warranty that just comes stock on it, but I put a price to that because it has some value. I then give it to them for free. In alarms, I would list every sensor or piece of equipment, and what it would normally cost, and then total up the whole system value. The bigger the total at the end, within reason, the better. You can also do this with monthly payments. If you can build the perceived value high enough, people will believe that the higher monthly price you give is the normal retail price.

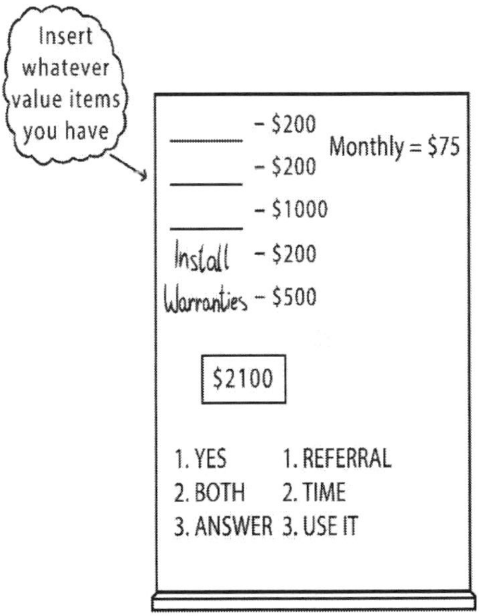

There is an art to this close, and a lot of it has to do with being unattached to whether or not they buy from you. When presenting the numbers, I always explain that these would be the normal costs if you were to call in and buy it or go through a different program. After getting to the total price, I like to present two options:

1) You can work with me and my program, and I'll show you what you get.

2) You can call the 1-800 number any time and your prices will look something like this.

Obviously, we make more money on this option, and we highly encourage it. They would tie your name to my area, and I would get the credit.

Something along those lines, but don't make anything up – just explain it in a way that option 2 isn't a terrible option, it's just going to cost them a heck of a lot more money.

I then go on to say, "I have three questions and three requirements, and these are extremely important to me and if you can't do these three things, no deal." This will put you in the driver's seat.

Questions:

1) Do you consider yourself a vocal person?

2) When would you use the system most? Day, Night? (Or whatever makes sense to put here)
3) What would be the main reason you would get this?

Requirements:

1) Refer people to me if they ask you about it, at the end I'll go over my referral program
2) Work with me and my time frame. I am not the type that goes back and forth back and forth begging people to do this. I just get these done as I go.

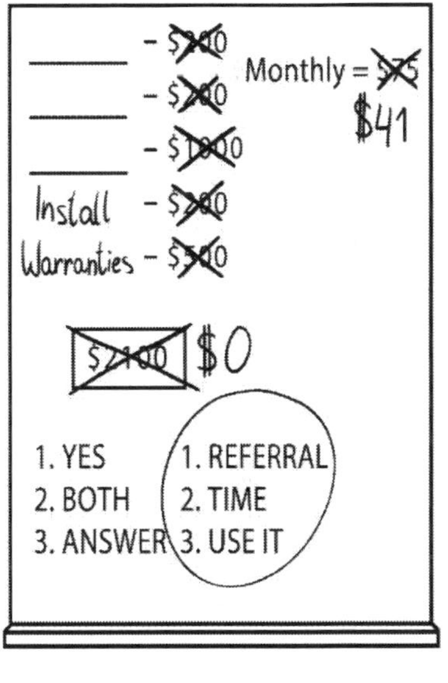

3) Use it! You would use it right?

If-Then Close – "If you do refer people to me, work with me and my time frame and use it, then I'll pay for your equipment, install, warranties… So, nothing upfront.

And all you pay is $41 per month...Does that sound fair?"

At this point you transition to paperwork!

I have used this in almost 100% of the deals that I have closed for the last 10 years. I have used it amongst different industries, and the psychology behind it works every time. After dropping the price, you should be speaking with a tone that makes them feel like they would be crazy if they didn't take you up on this. This will also give you leverage when people start to bring up things like, "Well I want to think about it," or "Sounds great, but can you just leave a card and we will get back to you," and so on. When they bring this up, you can say, "Yeah, like I said, I would be more than happy to leave you with the 1-800 number and then you can get this on your own time whenever you feel like it." You almost play the dumb card, as if you honestly could care less which they choose, you just want them to get your product or service, and there truly are 2 options. You get it now with me, or you call in and get it. This leaves the power totally up to the customer. They will fight you on this, and you HAVE to stay true to the program that you are offering – this will legitimize the offering. If you are wishy-washy and start to bend on giving them time and doing call backs, this close loses all of its weight.

You should also couple this close with the Give and Take Close (page 84) and the If Then Close (page 99). Make sure to ask for something in return. I love to leverage referrals, and ask them to work with me and my time frame.

NO JOKE, this is exactly what I have used for 10 years, and I have sold MILLIONS of dollars of product! Remember that this book is designed to give you the answers. COPY. PASTE.

Exercise:

List all of the features you can put a value to from your product or service, and put a dollar amount to them.

______________ = $______________
______________ = $______________
______________ = $______________
______________ = $______________
______________ = $______________
______________ = $______________
______________ = $______________

TOTAL = $

Write out your 3 Questions.

1) ______________________________

2) ______________________________

3) ______________________________

Write out your 3 Requirements.

1) ______________________________

2) ______________________________

3) ______________________________

Write out how you can leverage the Stack Close to create urgency in your deal.

____

____

____

____

____

____

____

____

Virgin Territory Close

Giving a better deal due to the fact that you're newer to the area.

Well coupled with the Knock on Your Door Close (page 119).

Often, when you're out pitching them, people have never heard of your company, and you can either use that to your advantage or to your disadvantage. Many reps assume that because they are in some super small company, people don't want to do business with them. They feel that the companies that advertise and spend millions of dollars to get their brand out have the competitive advantage. I would use that against the big companies, and leverage the fact that you don't do that type of advertising. Think about it this way – you are the company's marketers, and you are the least expensive and lowest risk, because most door-to-door salesmen get paid 100% commission, and the company only pays if revenue is created Companies that run TV commercials or have billboards have very few ways to track the conversion rates and ROI's on those types of marketing.

> "We don't spend millions of dollars on TV commercials and billboards, we come straight to you to earn your business, and give you a much better deal. We're investing in you, not in expensive advertising campaigns. Make sense?"

"We are fairly new to the area. To get the momentum rolling, we help the initial few homes with the costs so that we can get more future business, and hopefully you can point us in the right direction."

"We are looking for a few people that qualify for our initial program, to get the ball rolling in your neighborhood. There are a few qualifications that we have, but if you qualify, we take care of your costs _____."

"I have already done a few in your area (Bandwagon Close page. 51), which is why I'm giving you this deal. But over the next few days I'm going to be meeting with your other neighbors, and my company only limits me to ___ of these at this price, to get the ball rolling. I'll be back around over the next few weeks, and you're more than welcome to get it then, but I'm not guaranteeing the same price. Make sense?"

Leverage the fact that you are the little guy, and most people know that they can get better deals with the ma' and pa' shops. They might like the fact that you're local, or like the fact that you're fighting the behemoth companies.

You can leverage the fact that you're more intimate with your customers because you don't have millions of them. You can leverage the fact that you are really aggressive with your offering simply because you're new to the area, and that is what it is going to take to stir up some business.

Cheaper Isn't Always Better

Keep in mind that the cheapest price isn't always the answer. Some reps get super discouraged when they find competition that is cheaper, or is offering the same thing in their neighborhood. There will always be cheaper or better out there. That doesn't mean you can't sell what your company offers. You must find out what things you offer that make you and the customer the most excited, and hit on those things. At the end of the day, someone still buys a pair of $100 shoes even though they could find shoes for $5. There is value in the fact that you are their sales rep, and you deserve to get paid for making the transaction happen. Without you, no business would take place. Never feel guilty about how much you're making, or that you are ripping people off.

Exercise:

Write 2 ways you can use the Virgin Territory Close with your customers on the doors.

1) ______________________________________
____
____

2) ______________________________________
____
____

Write One way you can use the Virgin Territory Close with your customers in the home.

____
____
____
____
____
____
____

Why Close

Having a customer list, or stating all of the main reasons they would get your product or service.

> "What are the main reasons you would be getting______(solar, this system, etc.)?"
>
> "One of the things I always ask everyone to do is to write all of the reasons why they would be the best fit for my program."
>
> "One thing that we require is for you to write down three reasons why you would____ (go solar, protect your home, use ___, etc.)."

This is another great form of a tie down, and though some may find it obvious and simple, it works magic! Have them tell you why they want it, straight up. Sometimes you may need to give a few thought joggers, like: to save money, or to have a better watch on the home, or the convenience of a certain product. Keep egging them on to give you as many as they can come up with, but let *them* come up with things. You may have to sit in silence for a minute.

If you make it sound like you are requiring it as part of your qualification, it will make them come to you more. They may start to sell you on why they deserve your service or product, and why they are passionate about it. I can't say it enough – people like to buy, they don't like to be sold.

The best time to use this close is right before you go into the price. You get them in a state of appreciation, and make them want to buy. And then whatever the price is, it will be harder for them to combat, because they just listed all of the reasons why they wanted to do it.

Bonus Close:

Win-Win Close

- Explain what is in it for the customer, and what is in it for you.

We Lose
I Win, You Lose
You Win, I Lose
We Booth Win

If this gets lopsided, and it stops really making sense for you as a rep or for your company, explain that. Explain that you're obviously in the business of win-win, or no deal. Sometimes customers try to push you to a limit where it just doesn't make sense for you anymore. Share with them if they have passed that threshold.

> "As long as I can make this a win-win, let's do it."
>
> "What's in it for you ___________?
> What's in it for me is ___________.
> Does that sound fair?"
>
> "If it isn't a win-win, no deal."
>
> "At the end of the day, I gave you the farm. If I go any more, it isn't a win for me anymore, you want to make sure it's a win-win, right?"

Exercise:

Write 5 questions, starting with the word "WHY," to create a setting where the customer is in a position of buying, not being sold.

Why______________________________?

Why ______________________________?

Why ______________________________?

Why ______________________________?

Why ______________________________?

X Marks the Spot Close

Guiding the customer to exactly where to initial or sign.

Great paired with the Pen Close (page 149)

- "I just need your initials there and there."
- "Just sign right there..."
- "Can I borrow your finger?" (E-Signature)
- "Click the yellow box and just follow the prompt." (DocuSign)
- "You can use the auto generated signature or draw your own, which would you prefer?" (DocuSign)
- "This is just saying you're ok with us paying for the ___. Initial there."

Another common way to use this close is simply to leverage the spaces in your paperwork that don't have to do with signing. Often, you can just start by filling out the paperwork with their first and last name. Or, you can get some key information from them that would be important to move the sale forward. For example, in alarms:

> "Who would you want to put down as your emergency contact if the system was to go off, and they weren't able to get a hold of you?"

You would be able to start filling out the form, but it would be a softer transition into paperwork.

TONE

The key to getting signatures is being 100% sure of yourself. A lot of this actually has to do with your tone. You can either use an up tone, a neutral tone, or a down tone. When using this close, you want to make sure that you are using down tones, which imply more of a command than a question.

It is not what you say, but how you say it –80% of communication is meta-verbal. Including your body language, your appearance, your tone, your eye contact, your posture, your energy, your essence, and so on. You need to be like a chameleon, and adapt to what your customer is calling for.

Tone is all about how you end your sentence. There are really three tones that you can use, while saying the same thing, to get different points across.

1) Up-tone - This would sound like a question, express doubt, or leave things open ended.

2) Neutral - This creates more of a level conversation, where it is easy for you to go back and forth.

3) Down-tone - This is used more as a command, a statement of fact, or a demonstration of confidence and certainty.

Some people have very forceful personalities, and will walk all over the rep that is using more of the up-tone, because they sound more passive. If you have someone that is a “red” personality, you need to be equally assertive in response. If you have someone that is much softer, they may get turned off by you being the bull in the conversation.

Exercise:

Based on your paperwork process, write down 2-3 ways you can leverage your paperwork to close a deal.

Yes, Yes, Yes
Close

A series of small "yes" answers to get to the bigger yes.

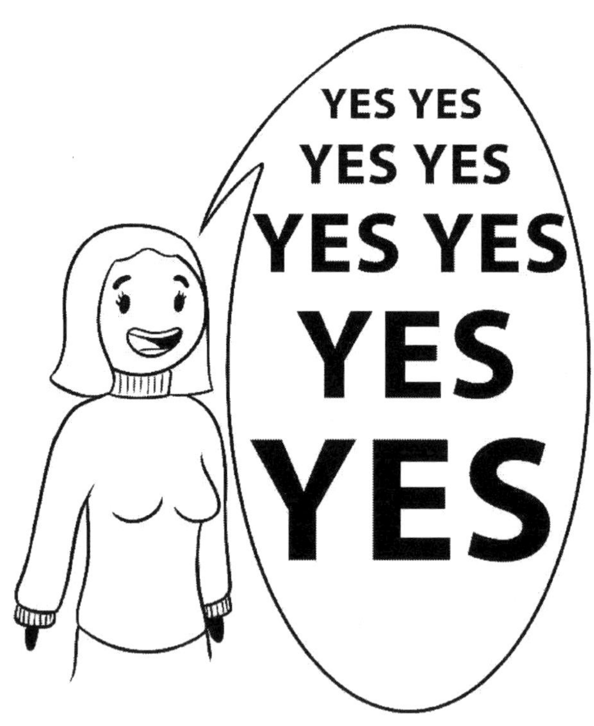

This works best when you have it fairly plotted out. You should pre-plan questions so that you know you can get your customer to get on the "Yes Train." The more yes's you can get, the more momentum you'll have going into your hard close.

Rep: "Have I answered all of your questions about how it works and what you'd be getting?"

Customer: "Yes."

Rep: "Is this something you could see yourself using?"

Customer: "Yes."

Rep: "If the price made sense, you would get it, right?"

Customer: "Yes."

Rep: (Show the price) “That’s it, does that sound fair so far?"

Customer: "Yes."

Rep: "Ok, the next step is ..."

This is just a simple example of how you could sequence a few questions in order to get multiple yes's. There are thousands of ways you can set this up, but the point of it is to program “yes” into their subconscious mind. I like to think of it as similar to this joke I used to play on people as a kid.

"Say Silk 10x as fast as you can...”

“Silk, Silk, Silk, Silk, Silk, Silk, Silk, Silk, Silk, Silk.”

“What do cows drink?"

Nine times out of ten, people will say milk.

This is also another form of NLP. You are embedding “yes” as many times as you can, so naturally a “yes” comes out, instead of a “no.” Our entire lives we hear the word “no” more than “yes.” We were taught no from a young age, and it is much easier for people not to do something, versus *to* do something. We must temporarily rewire their brains to make them feel that “yes” is the easier thing to do.

Exercise:

Write 10 different questions you can use throughout the sale from which you can get a little yes out of the customer.

1) ______________________________

2) ______________________________

3) ______________________________

4) ______________________________

5) ______________________________

6) ______________________________

7) ______________________________

8) ______________________________

9) ______________________________

10)______________________________

Z

Zero-Down Close

Building the price up, and then dropping it so that there's no cost upfront.

Similar to the Upsell Price Drop Close (page 193)

> "Hypothetically, if this didn't affect your budget today, would you do it?"
>
> "If you had to, how much would you be willing to put down today in order to get this started?"
>
> "How about nothing? Let's do this!"
>
> "The best part about all of this is that it literally doesn't cost you anything upfront! Your first payment isn't until next month. I just need your OK there, and there."
>
> "Normally the initial payment is X, but if we can get this done today, I'll take care of all your upfront costs. Deal?"

This won't work with every company or situation, but it is powerful to create a situation where the customer doesn't have to pay anything at the time of sale. People are naturally comfortable putting things on credit, most live paycheck to paycheck. They also don't usually have whatever you're pitching planned into their budgets. So, if you can create a scenario where they aren't immediately affected by buying, it will remove a potential barrier to them buying. Your job is to create the path of least resistance to purchasing. Sometimes, it is worth giving up a little commission to pay for their first payments, if that is what it calls for. This isn't a close you should use all the time, if it is eating into your commission, but try it a few times, and see what happens. I would put it in the category of a last-ditch close.

The thought that they are getting something for "free" makes people feel great. They love the bargains, they love the deal that you offer them. Some people might not even want your product or service, but if it's presented in the right way, they would simply feel bad if they passed up such a good deal. You want the customer to feel as if they would be sinning by not buying it, because the offering was so stinking good. If you can have this effect on a customer, you will be surprised how fast your sales will increase.

Exercise:

Write out what kind of scenario you could present that would be a zero-down situation for the customer. If you don't have one, what would make the path of least resistance for the customer to buy today? What are hurdles you can remove?

____

____

____

____

____

____

____

____

____

____

What questions could you ask the customer about your product or service that would help tee you up for the zero-down scenario? I.e., you are creating a situation where they dig themselves into a hole, and commit to your offering as long as it is zero-down.

Conclusion

Are you going to close more? It all depends on what you now do with all of this information. Please don't let me waste your time reading this book, and my time writing it, if you aren't going to go apply some of these closes and start making more money. Over the years in this industry, I have trained hundreds of reps, and have learned that there are only two types out there: 1) those that close and last in this industry, or 2) those that try this job out for a while, and hop around trying to make things work. But then eventually quit with an attitude of, "I'm just not a salesman." EVERYONE can be a salesman – it just takes work. This book has been laid out to really use the "copy-paste" strategy, not the "go figure everything out on your own" method that we sometimes deal with in this industry.

I hear a lot of excuses in this job for why people can't seem to make money. If, in your head, you are starting to come up with some right now, about why you aren't going to use these closes, or why they won't work for you, PLEASE STOP NOW! Those thoughts are coming from your unconscious natural tendency to justify why you are where you are. Our brain likes to feel safe, so we justify until we are OK with ourselves as we are, not the future BAD ASSES we could become. Newsflash for you – breaking through the normal you right now is the ONLY way for you to create massive growth!

Share the formulas that seem to be working best for you – we would love to hear about other closes that are working for you in this space. D2D is a collaborative learning platform for all things door to door and we look forward to hearing from you. Share this book only with those that are open to receiving knowledge, and are looking for a fishing pole, not a fish. The millennial generation, which is the lion share of reps in the door to door industry, are seeking easy handouts. This book was written for the hunter, the hungry, the leadership, and future of the D2D industry. We all know someone that fits that profile, so please send those you know a copy of the book, or tell them to go buy it. I have a mission to **UPLEVEL** the standard of excellence in the door to door industry, and the only way to accomplish that is by reaching the largest amount of people possible. Thank you for your support through this journey thus far, and I look forward to hearing feedback from you guys on Facebook, Instagram or YouTube.

D2DCON

D2Dcon is a yearly event designed where leaders in the D2D space come together to up-level the standards in the door-to-door industry. Leaders from every direct selling industry put their heads together to share best practices and learn from one another. We recognize the top talent from many industries every year honoring them with the “Golden Door Award.” Join us for a spectacular experience

D2Dcon.com